Professor Barclay was a distinguished scholar, an exceptionally gifted preacher and a regular broadcaster. His writings for the *British Weekly* were very popular and for twenty years from 1950 a full page every week was given to them. From 1963 until 1974 he was Professor of Divinity and Biblical Criticism at Glasgow University. He was a Member of the Advisory Committee working on the New English Bible and also a Member of the Apocrypha Panel of Translators. In 1975 he was appointed a Visiting Professor at the University of Strathclyde for a period of three years where he lectured on Ethics, and in the same year – jointly with the Rev. Professor James Stewart – he received the 1975 Citation from the American theological organization The Upper Room; the first time it has been awarded outside America. His extremely popular *Bible Study Notes* using his own translation of the New Testament have achieved a world-wide sale.

Professor Barclay died in January 1978.

WILLIAM BARCLAY

The Plain Man's Book of Prayers

Collins

FOUNT PAPERBACKS

First published in Fontana Books 1959
Reprinted in Fount Paperbacks March 1977
Twenty-fourth Impression June 1980

© William Barclay 1959

Made and printed in Great Britain by
William Collins Sons & Co Ltd Glasgow

CONTENTS

OURSELVES
AND OUR PRAYERS

IT SHOULD not be difficult to pray, for prayer is the most natural activity in the world. William James, the great American philosopher, said: " Many reasons have been given why we should not pray, whilst others are given why we should. But in all this very little is said of the reason why we do pray. The reason why we pray is simply that we cannot help praying." It is one of the most significant facts about the human situation that no tribe, however primitive, has been found whose people did not pray to such gods as they had. Prayer is not an acquired art; it is an instinct. In the times when life is too much for us, when we are strained beyond breaking-point, when we are tempted beyond the power to resist, when our minds are troubled, and our hearts are broken, then we pray.

If that be so, we may well ask: Why then do we need any help in prayer? If prayer is so natural, why cannot every man pray perfectly well for himself? Technique is not a word with very high and lofty associations, and yet there is a technique in everything. There can be nothing in this world so natural as breathing, and yet there is a technique in breathing; there is a right and a wrong way to breathe; and health will depend on which way we use. There are few activities so natural as walking; and yet there is a technique of walking. There is a right and a wrong way to walk, and it will make a very great difference which way we use.

We need to be taught how to use everything. It is quite possible for a man to possess something very precious, and yet to fail to get anything like the best out of it, because he is not using it aright. A man has to learn how to use a typewriter or an electric razor; he has to learn how to tune a violin or a television set; he has to learn how to drive a motor car; he has to learn even how to cook food, and how to cook it in such a way that he will get the maximum benefit from it.

The simplest and most natural actions have their technique, and a man has to learn how to use even his most precious possessions. It is not otherwise with prayer. There are many people who in their childhood years were taught to pray in a kind of a way; but bit by bit, as the years went on, they drifted out of the habit of prayer; and, if they considered the matter, and were honest about it, they would probably say that they stopped praying, because they had not found that prayer was any use. If that is so, the reason is that they were not praying in the right way; they had never learned and were never taught the technique of prayer; they possessed a very precious gift, but they did not know how to use it. Let us then look at some of the laws of prayer.

All prayer begins from the fact that God is even more ready to listen than we are to speak to Him, and even more ready to give than we are to ask. When we pray, we do not go to a grudging and an unwilling God. God, as Paul saw it, has given proof, unanswerable proof, of His generosity. " He that spared not His own Son, but delivered Him up for us all, how shall He not with Him also freely give us all things? " (Romans 8 : 32). There are two prayer parables which Jesus spoke to men; and the misunderstanding of them has done an infinite deal of harm. The one is the parable we call the Parable of the Friend at Midnight (Luke 11 : 5–8). It tells how a belated traveller arrived at a man's house. It was so late that the man had no food to set before him, and in the East hospitality is a sacred duty. So the man went along to his neighbour, although it was midnight, and knocked at his door in order to borrow bread. The neighbour was in bed, and at first refused to get up. But the man who needed bread knocked and knocked and knocked; he knocked with shameless persistence;

and at last the man in bed was forced to get up and give him what he needed. The second parable is the parable we call the Parable of the Unjust Judge (Luke 18 : 2–7). It tells how in a certain town there was a widow who wished for justice. In the same town there was an unjust judge. No one would ever have got a favourable verdict out of him without a handsome bribe, and that the widow could not bring, for she had no money. But she had one thing—she had persistence; and she kept coming back and back and back again, until the unjust judge gave her what she wanted for very weariness at her persistence. Often people take these parables to mean that, if we persist long enough in prayer, we will get what we want. If we batter at God's door long enough, if we badger God persistently enough, if we set up a bombardment and barrage of prayer, in the end God will succumb, and grant our request. That is not what these parables teach. A parable literally means *something which is laid alongside something else*. It comes from the two Greek words *para*, which means *beside*, and *ballein*, which means *to throw*. When we place two things alongside each other, we do so for the sake of comparison; but the point of the comparison may lie either in *resemblance* or in *contrast*. Many of Jesus' parables do work by resemblance, but this one works by contrast. In these parables God is not *likened* to a churlish and unwilling householder or to an unjust and stubborn judge; He is *contrasted* with such a person. Jesus is saying : If a churlish and unwilling householder will in the end give a persistent friend the bread he needs, if an unjust and stubborn judge will in the end give a widow the justice for which she pleads, *how much more* will God, who is a loving father, give us what we need ? That is the very thing which Jesus goes on to say. He bids us to ask that we may receive, to seek that we may find, to knock that it may be opened to us. If we, who are evil, know how to give good gifts to our children, *how much more* will our heavenly Father give us what is needful for life ? (Luke 11 : 13 ; Matthew 7 : 11).

Here is the great and precious truth on which all prayer depends. God is not some one from whom gifts and favours have to be unwillingly extracted; He is not some one whose defences have to be battered down, and whose resistance has to be sapped and undermined. God is more willing to give than we are to ask.

> *Come, my soul, thy suit prepare;*
> *Jesus loves to answer prayer;*
> *He Himself has bid thee pray,*
> *Therefore will not say thee nay.*
>
> *Thou art coming to a King;*
> *Large petitions with thee bring;*
> *For His grace and power are such,*
> *None can ever ask too much.*

But we cannot leave this matter here, and it is because it is so often left here that so many people drift out of the habit of prayer. We have said—and it is the basic truth of prayer—that God is a loving father who is more ready to give than we are to ask. Does this mean that we have only to pray in order to receive, and that God will give us everything that we ask? That is precisely what it does not mean, and it is here that we must grasp and understand the laws of prayer.

The first law of prayer is that *we must be honest in prayer*. Luther said that the first law of prayer is, "Don't lie to God." The great temptation in prayer is to become conventional, to pray in pious language for the things for which we know we ought to pray. But the truth is that at least sometimes no one would be more shocked than we would be, if our prayer was granted. We may pray for the giving up of some habit—without the slightest intention of giving it up. We may pray for some virtue or quality—without any real desire to possess it. We may pray to be made into a certain kind of person—when the last thing that we in fact want is to be changed, and when we are very well content to be as we are. The peril of prayer is pious and unmeaning platitudes. The danger of prayer is that we very correctly ask for " the right things," with no desire to receive them. That is lying to God. We cannot pray for that which we do not desire with our whole hearts. If there is something which we know we ought to desire, and we do not desire it, then our first step must be not to pray for it; that would be dishonest; but to confess that the holy desire which ought to be in our hearts is not there, and to ask God by His Spirit to put it there. There should be in our prayers an astringent honesty with ourselves, so that we may be honest with God, for God sees the secrets of our hearts, and God well knows when we are conventionally asking for blessings which we have no real desire to receive.

A second law of prayer follows naturally from this; *we must be very definite in prayer.* It is not enough to ask God's forgiveness, because we are wretched and miserable sinners. That is far too easy and too comfortable. We must name and confess our actual sins to God. It is not enough vaguely to thank God for all His gifts. We must specifically name the gifts for which we are giving thanks. It is not enough nebulously to ask God to make us good. We must ask for the particular things in which we know that we are lacking, and which we know that we need. Herein lies the great difficulty of prayer. *There can be no real prayer without self-examination.* And self-examination is difficult, exhausting, and, above all, shaming and humiliating. Many of us spend life running away from ourselves rather than facing ourselves. One of the great reasons why our prayers are not what they should be is that so few people will face the stern discipline of self-examination in the presence of God on which prayer is based. Prayer and self-examination go hand in hand.

But we cannot stop even here. Suppose we do have perfect faith in God as a loving and a generous father; suppose we are honest in prayer; suppose we do achieve the discipline of self-examination and the consequent definiteness in prayer; will we then receive anything for which we ask? There are still more laws which govern prayer and which we must always remember.

We must remember that we are bound up in the bundle of life. We are not single, detached, isolated units; we are part of a fellowship, a society, a community, whether we like it or not. Anything that we do necessarily affects other people. We are therefore bound to see that *God cannot grant a selfish request*. It may well happen that, if our prayer is granted, then some one else in some way suffers. It may well happen that to give us what we desire would deprive some one else of what he or she should have. We so often pray as if no one mattered but ourselves, as if we were the centre of the universe, as if life and all that is in it ought to be organised and adjusted for our special benefit. No prayer which is forgetful of others can ever be answered, as we wish it to be answered. Mankind is the family of God, and there can be no spoiled children, who get whatever they cry for, in God's family.

It is even more important to remember that *God always knows best*. Very often in our ignorance we pray for things which, if they were given to us, would not be to our ultimate and lasting good. It could not be otherwise. Because we are human beings the only thing which we can see is the present moment. We do not know what is going to happen a week, a day, an hour, even a moment ahead. We are like people who come into a cinema in the middle of a film; we have not seen the beginning; we do not know the end; and the happenings on the screen are a mystery to us. God alone sees all time, and, therefore, God alone knows what is good for us; and, for that very reason, God can often best answer our prayers by *not* giving us that for which we ask. There is nothing specially mysterious about this. It is a principle which we ourselves often observe with our own children. The child asks for something; we love the child, and our desire is for nothing but the child's happiness; and we know that, if the child were to get what he is asking for it would not be good for him, and might even be a danger to him, and do him an injury. It is so with us and God. We do not need to be very old to be able to look back on life, and to see that, if certain of our prayers had been granted, life would be infinitely poorer than it is today. The fact is that there is no such thing as unanswered prayer. It has been wisely said that God has three answers to our prayers. Sometimes God says, " Yes ! " Sometimes God says, " No ! " Sometimes God says, " Wait ! " From even our own limited experience of life it must surely be easy to see that, if God granted all our prayers, it would be very far from being for our ultimate good, and that God must often give us the true answer to our prayers by withholding what we ask. At the end of the day we shall see that there is no such thing as unanswered prayer, for God in His wisdom sends us the answer, not which our ignorance desires, but which His love and knowledge knows to be best.

There is a further inevitable law of prayer. *God will not do for us that which we can do for ourselves.* Prayer is not an easy way out to save us from trouble. Prayer is not a means of evading our own responsibilities and of escaping our own allotted toil. We may put this in another way. No sooner have we prayed than we must set out to make our own prayers come true; prayer is the cooperation of our effort with the grace of God. It is when we make our greatest effort that God sends His greatest answer. But, when we do make that effort, God sends His answer without fail. Suppose there is a student who has done little or none of the work required for an examination; suppose he has idled away his time, or has given it to things which are good enough in themselves, but which are not the things which he ought to have been doing; suppose that then on the morning of the examination he enters the examination hall, picks up the examination paper, and finds that he cannot answer the prescribed questions; then suppose that he bows his head and prays devoutly, " O God, help me to pass this examination." This is not a real prayer. To answer it would be to reward laziness and to approve time given to the wrong things. But, suppose this student to have worked faithfully ; suppose him to have a nervous and self-distrustful temperament ; suppose him to know his work, and yet to be from the nervous point of view a bad examinee ; suppose him then to bow his head and to pray, " O God, you know how hard I have worked ; and you know how easily I get excited and nervous ; calm me and keep me calm ; and help me to do justice to myself and to the work that I have done." That is a prayer which, if it is prayed in humble trust, can and will be answered. In prayer the enabling grace of God comes to meet the earnest effort of man.

There is little point in praying to be enabled to overcome some temptation, and then in flirting with that temptation, in playing with fire, and in putting oneself in the very position in which the temptation can exert all its fascination. There is little point in praying that God will convert the heathen, and then in refusing to give sixpence a week to make it possible to bring the gospel to the heathen. There is little point in praying that the sorrowing may be comforted and the lonely cheered, unless we ourselves set out to bring comfort and cheer to the sad and the neglected in our own sphere. There is little point in praying for our home and for our loved ones, and in going on being as selfish and inconsiderate as we have been. If we are ill, and we go to a doctor, the doctor will prescribe some medicine, some diet, some course of treatment, some method of exercise ; and, unless we agree to make the necessary effort of will to carry out the doctor's instructions, we might as well never have consulted him. The doctor's knowledge and our obedient effort and self-discipline must cooperate towards our cure. It is not otherwise with prayer. Prayer would be an evil rather than a blessing, if it were only a way of getting God to do what we ourselves will not make the effort to do. God does not do things for us; He enables us to do them for ourselves. God's word to Ezekiel was, " Son of man, stand on thy feet and I will speak to thee " (Ezekiel 2 : 1). God answers the prayer of the man who is spiritually, mentally and physically stripped for action, but not the prayer of the man who regards life in terms of the arm-chair. Many of our prayers would be answered if we were prepared with God's help to make the effort to make them come true.

There is still another law of prayer which we must always remember. *Prayer moves within the natural laws which govern life.* When we think of it, this is a necessity. The characteristic of this world is that it is a dependable world; if the laws which govern it were erratically suspended, it would cease to be an order and become a chaos. Suppose a man accidentally to fall from the fortieth floor window of a New York sky-scraper; suppose him to be a good and devout man and a firm believer in prayer; suppose him, as he passes the twentieth floor in his downward descent, to pray, " O God, stop me falling." That is a prayer which cannot be answered, because in that moment that man is in the grip of the law of gravity, and to suspend the law of gravity would be to put an end, not to his fall, but to the world in general.

A very important conclusion follows from this. Prayer does not normally promise or achieve release from some situation; it brings power and endurance to meet and to overcome that situation. In the Garden of Gethsemane Jesus prayed, if it was God's will, to be released from the Cross. He was not released from the Cross, but He was given power to endure the Cross.

Let us take a very simple example of this. It is sometimes the custom to pray for good weather for the day of a children's outing or the like. Such a prayer is quite wrong. It is not prayer but atmospheric conditions which determine the weather, and in any event the farmer may well be praying for rain for his parched crops. The correct prayer in such conditions is that we may be enabled to enjoy the day with glad cheerfulness, hail, rain or shine.

The basic mistake which so many people make about prayer is that almost instinctively they regard prayer as a means of escape from a situation; and prayer is not primarily a means of escape, it is a means of conquest. The laws of life are not relaxed for us by prayer, but through prayer there comes the strength and power to endure and to overcome any situation.

We must now step aside from these great laws and principles of prayer to look at the methods of prayer.

There are five great divisions of prayer. There is *Invocation*. Invocation means *calling* or *inviting in*. But we must be clear what we mean by invocation. Invocation does not mean that we invite God to be present at our prayers, for God is everywhere and always present. It is far truer that in invocation we ask God to help us to realise that He is already with us, and to make us aware and conscious of His presence. God is not some distant stranger who has to be invited and persuaded into meeting with us; He is " closer to us than breathing and nearer than hands and feet," as Tennyson said. There is an unwritten saying of Jesus, which is not in the Gospels but which is very beautiful: " Wherever there are two, they are not without God, and wherever there is one alone, I say I am with him. Raise the stone, and thou shalt find me; cleave the wood and there I am." When the mason is working with the stone, or the carpenter with the wood, Jesus Christ is there. In invocation we remind ourselves that God is here.

There is *Confession*. In confession we tell God of our sins and our mistakes; we tell Him that we are truly sorry for them; and we ask His forgiveness for them. Two things are necessary in confession, two things which go hand in hand. There are necessary searching self-examination and uncompromising honesty with ourselves. There is a kind of folly which seeks to hide things not only from our fellow-men, but even from ourselves and from God. But God is the searcher of the hearts of men, the One who understands our thoughts afar off, the One from whom nothing is hidden or concealed. Maybe we ask: " If God knows it all already, why should I have to tell Him about it? If God loves me, and desires above all things to forgive me, why do I have to ask His forgiveness? " We must think in human terms, for they are the only terms in which we can think. When a child does something wrong, the parent knows it. The parent wants above all things to forgive, and the parent knows that the child is sorry for what he has done. But in spite of all that there is an unseen barrier between parent and child until the child comes of his own accord, and says, " I'm sorry I was bad." Then the barrier is down, and love is in the sunshine again. It is so with us and God. " If we confess our sins, He is faithful and just to forgive us our sins, and to cleanse us from all unrighteousness " (I John 1 : 9). There is one thing still to add. Confession without amendment is a sadly truncated thing. We must use the forgiving love of God not as a comfortable excuse for sinning, but as an inescapable challenge and obligation to goodness. The child says, " I'm sorry. I'll try to be better." And we must say the same.

There is *Thanksgiving*. Thanksgiving is the outcome of the natural gratitude of the heart. There are three kinds of thanksgiving. There is the thanksgiving for Jesus Christ, God's greatest and best gift to men. There is the thanksgiving for all the means of grace and for all the great joys and wonders of life, and for all the gifts of God which have helped us to meet the great moments of life. But there is a third kind of thanksgiving. One of the great dangers of life is that we should take people or things for granted. In life there are people who have become part of our lives; they are woven into the structure of life. And the danger is that we should regard them as no more than part of the landscape, part of the essential background of life. There are gifts which come to us so regularly day by day that we forget that they are gifts. And there must be thanksgiving for these things. When we think of what life would be like without the people and the things which are part of everyday life, then the whole day is not long enough to give thanks for them to God.

There is *Petition*. Petition is that part of prayer in which we ask God for the things which we need for life and living. Petition is born of a sense of our own insufficiency and a realisation of the all-sufficiency of God. Here again there is need for self-examination, because a man must realise his own need of help and healing before he is able to ask for them. Especially in petition prayer is the greatest test and touchstone in the world. In petition we take our hopes and dreams and desires to God. Whenever a thing is laid in the presence of God, its true character is at once made clear. Sometimes when we lay something in the presence of God, we see its unimportance. It often happens that, when we lay before God something which was worrying us, or something on which we had set our heart, it falls into its proper proportion, and we see that it does not matter so much after all. Sometimes when we lay a thing before God, we see how impossible it is that we should ask for it, and how wrong it is that we should desire it. One of the greatest tests of anything is—Can I pray for it? Sometimes when we lay a thing before God, we see that indeed this is something on which we may truly set our hearts and towards which we may truly direct our efforts and our lives. In petition we take the needs of life and spread them before God.

In this too we may ask the question, If God already in His wisdom knows what is good for me, and if God already in His love is even more willing to give than I am to ask, why must I ask at all? Why should I not simply leave it to God to give? Once again we must think in human terms. We may know what is good for a child or a young person or a loved one. We may be willing to give it even at the price of sacrifice. But we cannot give it until it will be accepted; we cannot give it until it is asked; we cannot give it until they tell us that they wish to receive it. It is so with us and God. One of the great wonders about God is His respect for the rights of human personality. God does not force His gifts upon us. He waits for us to tell Him that we are willing to receive them. And, therefore, in petition, we do not so much tell God what we want; rather we ask Him to give what He wills, and what He knows is best.

There is *Intercession*. In intercession we take the needs of the world and bring them to God for His blessing and His help. We remember before God those in illness and in distress of mind and all those whom we know specially to need God's blessing. In particular in intercession we ask God's blessing and God's keeping for our nearest and our dearest. It will always bring us comfort and peace of mind to leave those whom we love in the strong hands of God.

We began at the very beginning by saying that prayer is the most natural activity in the world. Since that is so, prayer should be made perfectly naturally. There is no one right position in which to pray. It does not matter whether we kneel, or stand, or sit, or lie. There is only one necessity; we should be in a position in which we are not conscious of our bodies at all. Any bodily crampedness or discomfort takes our thoughts away from what we are doing. We must find for ourselves the position in which we most easily pray.

It is even more important to remember that there is no special language in which to pray. We do not need to use biblical or prayer-book language; we do not need to use "Thou's" and "Thee's" We can talk to God as easily and as naturally as we talk to our closest friend, because God is our closest friend. It is told that there was once a man who wished very much to pray, but he did not know how he ought to begin. A wise friend said to him: "Sit down alone in your room. Put an empty chair opposite you. Imagine to yourself that Jesus is sitting in that chair. And talk to him as you would to the closest friend you have." God is not looking for perfect English style, or even for perfect grammar.

God is not caring whether or not we speak to him in perfectly phrased sentences. All that God wants is that we should speak to Him. Formalities of position and formalities of language mean nothing to God. He wants us to feel at home in His presence, and to talk to Him like a friend.

Because God is our friend, there is one thing we ought specially to remember about prayer. One of the sad things about our attitude to prayer is that so many of us connect prayer with the emergencies and the crises of life. When we are in trouble, when death and sorrow come, when there is illness and life is in danger, when there is worry and anxiety, when we are separated from those we love, then we pray. But when life is ordinary and things are going smoothly, when the sun is shining and the weather is calm, we forget to pray. When we act like that, it is as if we only remembered our best friend when we were in trouble and when we wanted to make use of Him. It is inevitable that there will be times when prayer is more intense than at other times; but prayer should be for us a constant thing. " A man, sir," said Dr Johnson, " should keep his friendship in constant repair." Our friendship with God should be a daily and a constant thing. Bertram Pollock was at one time Bishop of Norwich; and the life of a Bishop is a very busy life. In the memoir which she wrote of him his wife tells how every day in life he had certain hours set apart for prayer. No matter who came to see him at such times, he would say, " Put him in an anteroom and tell him to wait. I have an appointment with God." We should have our appointment each day with God; that engagement should be a priority engagement which nothing is allowed to break. There is something shameful in going to a friend only when we need him and when we want to get something out of him; and there is something shameful in treating God as some one to be made use of only when we are in trouble and when life goes wrong. In sunshine and in shadow we should have our times with God.

We have left the most important thing of all to the end. We have been speaking all the time so far as if prayer were always talking to God. But prayer is not a monologue in which we do all the talking; prayer is listening even more than it is talking. The highest form of prayer is silence when we wait on God and listen to God. We have a low view of prayer if we regard prayer as a way of telling God what we want Him to do; prayer is even more listening to God, as He tells us what He wants us to do. Prayer is not a way of making use of God; prayer is a way of offering ourselves to God in order that He should be able to make use of us. It may be that one of our great faults in prayer is that we talk too much and listen too little. When prayer is at its highest we wait in silence for God's voice to us; we linger in His presence for His peace and His power to flow over us and around us; we lean back in His everlasting arms and feel the serenity of perfect security in Him.

If we remember these things, prayer will not be a grim duty or a dull routine or a conventional duty; it will be the greatest thing in life, for in its power we shall find that we will emerge triumphantly from anything that life can do to us.

This little book is offered as a help to those who wish to pray. There are prayers for morning and evening in the family circle. And there are prayers, some of them much more personal, for the special occasions which arise in life. Those who use this book will naturally wish to insert into these prayers their own prayers which rise from their own situation, and from their own needs and desires. And this book will have fulfilled its aim when those who use it will discard it, and will use it no longer, but will speak to God in their own words, and in their own way.

I send out this book as a help for those who wish to pray within the family circle and for themselves. And it is my own prayer that those who use it will finally come not to need its help any more.

PRAYERS WITH BIBLE READINGS
FOR THIRTY DAYS

In the Morning

O God, our Father, who ever makest the light to shine out of the darkness, we thank Thee for waking us to see the light of this new day. Grant unto us to waste none of its hours; to soil none of its moments; to neglect none of its opportunities; to fail in none of its duties. And bring us to the evening time undefeated by any temptation, at peace with ourselves, at peace with our fellow-men, and at peace with Thee. This we ask for Thy love's sake. AMEN.

In the Evening

O God, our Father, we thank Thee for this day which is passing from us now.

For any glimpse of beauty we have seen;
For any echo of Thy truth that we have heard;
For any kindness that we have received;
For any good that we have been enabled to do;
And for any temptation which Thou didst give us grace to overcome:
We thank Thee, O God.

We ask Thy forgiveness for anything which has spoiled and marred this day.
For any word which now we wish that we had never spoken;
For any deed which now we wish that we had never done;

For everything which makes us ashamed when we
    remember it;
Forgive us, O God.

Eternal God, who givest us the day for work and the
    night for rest, grant unto us, as we go to rest, a good
    night's sleep; and wake us refreshed on the morrow,
    better able to serve Thee and to serve our fellow-men.
    This we ask, through Jesus Christ our Lord.

Daily Reading

MATTHEW 5: 1–12

AND SEEING the multitudes, he went up into a mountain:
and when he was set, his disciples came unto him: and
he opened his mouth, and taught them, saying, Blessed
are the poor in spirit for theirs is the kingdom of heaven.
Blessed are they that mourn: for they shall be comforted.
Blessed are the meek: for they shall inherit the earth.
Blessed are they which do hunger and thirst after righteousness: for they shall be filled. Blessed are the merciful: for they shall obtain mercy. Blessed are the pure
in heart: for they shall see God. Blessed are the
peacemakers: for they shall be called the children of
God. Blessed are they which are persecuted for righteousness' sake: for theirs is the kingdom of heaven.
Blessed are ye, when men shall revile you, and persecute
you, and shall say all manner of evil against you falsely,
for my sake. Rejoice, and be exceeding glad: for great
is your reward in heaven: for so persecuted they the
prophets which were before you.

In the Morning

O God, our Father, bless us and keep us all through today.

At our work, make us diligent, ever showing ourselves to be workmen who have no need to be ashamed.
In our pleasure, help us to find delight only in such things as bring no regrets to follow.
In our homes, make us kind and considerate, ever trying to make the work of others easier, and not harder.
In our dealings with our fellow-men, make us courteous and kindly.
In our dealings with ourselves, make us honest to face the truth.

And in every moment of this day make us ever to remember that Thou, God, seest us, and that in Thee we live and move and have our being. So grant that we may do nothing which would bring shame to ourselves, grief to those who love us, and sorrow to Thee : through Jesus Christ our Lord. AMEN.

In the Evening

O God, our Father, who hast bidden us to pray for all men, we remember at evening time those who specially need our prayers.

Bless those who are lonely, and who feel their loneliness worst of all at evening time.
Bless those who are sad, and who at evening feel most of all the absence of some one whom they loved, and lost awhile.
Bless those who are ill, and who will not sleep this

night; and those who this night will wake to ease the sufferer's pain.

Bless those who have no home, and no family circle to call their own.

O God, who art everywhere present, bless this our home, and help us to remember that Jesus is always our unseen guest, and so help us never in this place to do or to say anything which would make Him sad to see.

Keep us this night in the dark hours, and grant us kindly sleep, and make us to feel around us and about us the clasp of the everlasting arms, which will never let us go: through Jesus Christ our Lord.   AMEN.

Daily Reading

PSALM 145: 9–16

THE LORD is good to all: and his tender mercies are over all his works.

All thy works shall praise thee, O Lord; and thy saints shall bless thee.

They shall speak of the glory of thy kingdom, and talk of thy power;

To make known to the sons of men his mighty acts, and the glorious majesty of his kingdom.

Thy kingdom is an everlasting kingdom, and thy dominion endureth throughout all generations.

The Lord upholdeth all that fall, and raiseth up all those that be bowed down.

The eyes of all wait upon thee; and thou givest them their meat in due season.

Thou openest thine hand, and satisfiest the desire of every living thing.

In the Morning

O God, our Father, who hast bidden us to live in fellowship with one another, keep us from everything which would make us difficult to live with today.

Help us never thoughtlessly or deliberately to speak in such a way that we would hurt another's feelings, or wound another's heart.

Keep us from all impatience, from all irritability, and from a temper which is too quick.

Keep us from eyes which are focused to find fault and from a tongue which is tuned to criticise.

Keep us from being touchy, and quick to take offence, and slow to forget it.

Help us not to be stubborn and obstinate, and keep us from the selfishness which can see nothing but its own point of view, and which wants nothing but its own way.

Grant unto us all through this day something of the grace and beauty which shone upon our blessed Lord.

Hear this our prayer, for Thy love's sake.   AMEN.

In the Evening

Eternal God, who didst give us this day, and who now at evening time art taking it back to Thyself, forgive us for all which today we did not do.

Forgive us for any word of comfort, of praise, of thanks, which we might have spoken, and did not speak.

Forgive us for any help we might have given to some one in need, and did not give.

Forgive us if today we have made things more difficult
for anyone.

Forgive us if by word or action we have set a bad example
to any one, and have made it easier for another to go
wrong.

Forgive us if today we have been disloyal to any friend,
or if we have hurt the hearts of those whom above all
we ought to cherish.

Grant us this night Thy gift of sleep; and grant us grace
that tomorrow we may walk more close to Thee:
through Jesus Christ our Lord.   AMEN.

Daily Reading

LUKE 12: 15–21

AND HE said unto them, Take heed, and beware of
covetousness: for a man's life consisteth not in the
abundance of the things which he possesseth. And he
spake a parable unto them, saying, The ground of a
certain rich man brought forth plentifully: and he
thought within himself, saying, What shall I do, because
I have no room where to bestow my fruits? And he
said, This will I do: I will pull down my barns, and
build greater; and there will I bestow all my fruits and
my goods. And I will say to my soul, Soul, thou hast
much goods laid up for many years; take thine ease,
eat, drink, and be merry. But God said unto him, Thou
fool, this night thy soul shall be required of thee: then
whose shall those things be, which thou hast provided?
So is he that layeth up treasure for himself, and is not
rich toward God.

In the Morning

O God, our Creator and our Father, who hast given unto us the gift of life, bless us this day as we go to the work which has been given unto us to do.

We give Thee thanks for our work, and for the health to do it.

We thank Thee for skill of hand, for accuracy of eye and mind and brain, to earn a living and to do the work of a house and home.

We thank Thee for the friends and the comrades whom Thou hast given to us, for those in whose company joys are doubly dear, and in whose presence sorrow's pain is soothed.

Help us today to be so cheerful, that it may make others happier to meet us.

Help us to be so true to Thee, that we may be a strength to others who are tempted.

O Lord Jesus, we have begun the day with Thee; grant that Thy reflection may be upon us throughout all its hours. This we ask for Thy love's sake.   AMEN.

In the Evening

O God, the Giver of every good gift, there is so much for which we ought to give Thee thanks.

We thank Thee for going out in the morning, and for coming home at evening time.

We thank Thee for the joy of work, and for all clean pleasures which rest our body and relax our mind.

We thank Thee for the light of the morning, and for the dark of the night.

We thank Thee for the day with all its duties and its tasks, and for the night and kindly sleep.

Grant unto us this night a mind at rest.

Grant that we may forget our worries in the peace that passeth understanding; and that we may lose our anxieties in the certainty that neither we nor those we love can drift beyond Thy love and care.

Grant unto us to sleep in peace and to wake in strength, because we sleep and wake in Thee; through Jesus Christ our Lord.   AMEN.

Daily Reading

MATTHEW 5: 13–16

YE are the salt of the earth : but if the salt have lost his savour, wherewith shall it be salted? it is thenceforth good for nothing, but to be cast out, and to be trodden under foot of men. Ye are the light of the world. A city that is set on a hill cannot be hid. Neither do men light a candle, and put it under a bushel, but on a candlestick ; and it giveth light unto all that are in the house. Let your light so shine before men, that they may see your good works, and glorify your Father which is in heaven.

FIFTH DAY

In the Morning

Eternal and everblessed God, who art the Lord of all good life, we do not know what will come to us and what will happen to us today. Whatever comes to us, be Thou with us to guide and to strengthen, to comfort and control.

If temptation comes to us, give us grace to overcome evil and to do the right.

If we have to make important decisions, give us grace ever to choose the right way, and to refuse the wrong way.

If it will be difficult to witness for Thee, give us courage never to be ashamed to show whose we are and whom we serve.

If things go well with us, keep us from all pride, and keep us from thinking that we do not need Thee.

If we shall know sorrow, failure, disappointment, loss, keep us from all despair, and help us never to give in.

O Thou who art the Light of the World, be Thou with us today, whatever light may shine or shadow fall, that we may ever live and walk as children of the light: through Jesus Christ our Lord. AMEN.

In the Evening

O God, our Father, who hast given us a life to live, and a task to do, bless us at eventide.

Forgive us for the things which we have left half done today, and for the things which we have not even begun.

Forgive us for the plans that we made, and did not carry out; and for the dreams which are still only dreams.

Forgive us for the promises which we made to Thee and to our fellow-men, and did not keep.

O God, our Father, bless those who this night specially need Thy blessing.

Bless those on journeys by sea and land and air; those who this night will lie down in hunger and in cold; those who are in prison and in disgrace; those who are ill and who will not sleep tonight; those who are sad and for whom the slow, dark hours are very lonely.

Bless each one of us, and be with us through this night, and stay with us until the day shall break and all the shadows flee away: through Jesus Christ our Lord.

Daily Reading

PSALM 23

THE LORD is my shepherd; I shall not want.

He maketh me to lie down in green pastures: he leadeth me beside the still waters.

He restoreth my soul: he leadeth me in the paths of righteousness for his name's sake.

Yea, though I walk through the valley of the shadow of death, I will fear no evil: for thou art with me; thy rod and thy staff comfort me.

Thou preparest a table before me in the presence of mine enemies: thou anointest my head with oil; my cup runneth over.

Surely goodness and mercy shall follow me all the days of my life: and I will dwell in the house of the Lord for ever.

In the Morning

O God, our Father, who hast bidden us to be lights in this dark world, help us throughout all this day to be a help and an example to all whom we meet.

Help us to bring comfort to those in sorrow, and strength to those who are tempted.

Help us to bring courage to those who are afraid, and guidance to those who do not know what to do.

Help us to bring cheer to those who are discouraged, and encouragement to those who are depressed.

And grant that, as we move among men and women this day, they may catch a glimpse in us of the Master, whose we are and whom we seek to serve. This we ask for Thy love's sake. AMEN.

In the Evening

Eternal and everblessed God, we give Thee thanks, as this day comes to an end, for those who mean so much to us, and without whom life could never be the same.

We thank Thee for those to whom we can go at any time, and never feel a nuisance.

We thank Thee for those to whom we can go when we are tired, knowing that they have, for weary feet, the gift of rest.

We thank Thee for those with whom we can talk, and keep nothing back, knowing that they will not laugh at our dreams or mock at our failures.

We thank Thee for those in whose presence it is easier to be good.

We thank Thee for those in whose company joys are doubly dear, and sorrow's bitterness is soothed.

We thank Thee for those who by their warning, their counsel, and their rebuke have kept us from mistakes we might have made, and sins we might have committed.

And above all we thank Thee for Jesus, the pattern of our lives, the Lord of our hearts, and the Saviour of our souls.

Accept this our thanksgiving, and grant us tonight a good night's rest: through Jesus Christ our Lord.

AMEN.

Daily Reading

PSALM 121

I WILL lift up mine eyes unto the hills, from whence cometh my help.

My help cometh from the Lord, which made heaven and earth.

He will not suffer thy foot to be moved: he that keepeth thee will not slumber.

Behold, he that keepeth Israel shall neither slumber nor sleep.

The Lord is thy keeper: the Lord is thy shade upon thy right hand.

The sun shall not smite thee by day, nor the moon by night.

The Lord shall preserve thee from all evil: he shall preserve thy soul.

The Lord shall preserve thy going out and thy coming in from this time forth, and even for evermore.

In the Morning

O God, our Father, who dost desire us to love and to
serve one another, and who hast created us for fellowship with Thee and with our fellow-men, grant unto
us all through this day the gifts and the graces which
will make us easy to live with.

Grant us courtesy, that we may live every moment as if
we were living at the court of the King.

Grant us tolerance, that we may not be so quick to
condemn what we do not like and what we do not
understand.

Grant unto us considerateness, that we may think of the
feelings of others even more than of our own.

Grant unto us kindliness, that we may miss no opportunity to help, to cheer, to comfort and to encourage
a brother man.

Grant unto us honesty, that our work may be our best,
whether there is anyone to see it or not.

Grant unto us so to live this day that the world may be a
happier place because we passed through it; through
Jesus Christ our Lord.   AMEN.

In the Evening

O God, our Father, we thank Thee that Thou didst
keep us this day in our going out and in our coming
in.

We thank Thee that Thou didst enable us to do our
work, and that Thou didst keep us in safety on our
journey to our work, and on the busy city streets.

We thank Thee for things to do, for friends to meet, and for all good pleasures to enjoy.

We thank Thee for clothes to wear, for food to eat, for a home from which we go out and to which at evening time we return, and for loved ones who ever care for us and take thought for all things for our comfort.

Grant that we may never take for granted all the things which come to us so regularly each day, but that we may ever remember Thee, the Giver of every good and perfect gift.

So grant unto us this night to lay ourselves down in gratitude, and on the morrow to wake in resolution to serve Thee better for all Thy love to us: through Jesus Christ our Lord.   AMEN.

Daily Reading

MATTHEW 6: 9-15

AFTER THIS manner therefore pray ye: Our Father which art in heaven, Hallowed be thy name. Thy kingdom come. Thy will be done in earth, as it is in heaven. Give us this day our daily bread. And forgive us our debts, as we forgive our debtors. And lead us not into temptation, but deliver us from evil: For thine is the kingdom, and the power, and the glory, for ever. Amen.

For if ye forgive men their trespasses, your heavenly Father will also forgive you: but if ye forgive not men their trespasses, neither will your Father forgive your trespasses.

In the Morning

O God, our Father, before we go out on the duties and the tasks of this day, we ask Thee to direct, to control, and to guide us all through its hours.

Grant that today we may never for one moment forget Thy presence.

Grant that we may take no step, and that we may come to no decision, without Thy guidance, and that, before we act, we may ever seek to find Thy will for us.

Be on our lips, that we may speak no evil word.

Be in our eyes, that they may never linger on any forbidden thing.

Be on our hands, that we may do our own work with diligence, and serve the needs of others with eagerness.

Be in our minds, that no soiled or bitter thought may gain an entry to them.

Be in our hearts, that they may be warm with love for Thee, and for our fellow-men.

Help us to begin, to continue, and to end this day in Thee: through Jesus Christ our Lord.   AMEN.

In the Evening

Eternal and everblessed God, help us this night to lay ourselves down in peace.

Give us that peace of mind, which comes from casting all our burdens upon Thee, and from leaving ourselves and our loved ones entirely to Thy care.

Give us that peace, which comes from being in perfect personal relationships with our fellow men, with no misunderstandings between us and them, and with no bitterness to anyone.

Give us the peace of sins forgiven, which comes from the certainty that, through Jesus Christ, there is no barrier between ourselves and Thee.

And, above all, give us the peace of Thy presence, and the certainty that in light and in dark Thou wilt never leave us, nor forsake us, and that Thou wilt never let us go: through Jesus Christ our Lord.

AMEN.

Daily Reading

PSALM 43

JUDGE ME, O God, and plead my cause against an ungodly nation: O deliver me from the deceitful and unjust man.

For thou art the God of my strength: why dost thou cast me off? why go I mourning because of the oppression of the enemy?

O send out thy light and thy truth: let them lead me; let them bring me unto thy holy hill, and to thy tabernacles.

Then will I go unto the altar of God, unto God my exceeding joy: yea, upon the harp will I praise thee, O God my God.

Why are thou cast down, O my soul? and why art thou disquieted within me? hope in God: for I shall yet praise him, who is the health of my countenance, and my God.

In the Morning

O God, our Father, help us all through this day so to live that we may bring help to others, credit to ourselves and to the name we bear, and joy to those who love us, and to Thee.

Help us to be,
Cheerful when things go wrong;
Persevering when things are difficult;
Serene when things are irritating.

Enable us to be,
Helpful to those in difficulties;
Kind to those in need;
Sympathetic to those whose hearts are sore and sad.

Grant that,
Nothing may make us lose our temper;
Nothing may take away our joy;
Nothing may ruffle our peace;
Nothing may make us bitter towards any man.

So grant that all through this day all with whom we work, and all whom we meet, may see in us the reflection of the Master, whose we are, and whom we seek to serve. This we ask for Thy love's sake.

AMEN.

In the Evening

Eternal God, this night we thank Thee for Thy good hand upon us through all this day.

We thank Thee that Thou hast enabled us to do our
work, and to earn a living for ourselves and for those
we love.

We thank Thee for the voice within us, which spoke to
us when we were tempted to do wrong, and for the
grace which kept us right.

We thank Thee for Thy protecting power, which has
brought us in safety to this evening hour.

O God, with whom is forgiveness, forgive us, if today we
have failed a friend, hurt a loved one, shamed ourselves, and grieved Thee.

Forgive us if we have been slack in duty to our fellow-
men, or careless in remembering Thee.

And now grant unto us to sleep in peace, and to wake in
strength: through Jesus Christ our Lord.   AMEN.

Daily Reading

MATTHEW 9: 10-13

AND IT came to pass, as Jesus sat at meat in the house,
behold, many publicans and sinners came and sat down
with him and his disciples. And when the Pharisees
saw it, they said unto his disciples, Why eateth your
Master with publicans and sinners? But when Jesus
heard that, he said unto them, They that be whole need
not a physician, but they that are sick. But go ye and
learn what that meaneth, I will have mercy and not
sacrifice: for I am not come to call the righteous, but
sinners to repentance.

In the Morning

O God, our Father, save us this day from all the sins into which we so easily and so continually fall.

Save us from demanding standards from others which we never even try to satisfy ourselves.

Save us from being very easy on ourselves and very hard on others.

Save us from making excuses for things in ourselves which in others we would condemn.

Save us from being wide-open-eyed to the faults of others, and blind to our own.

Save us from taking for granted all that our loved ones do for us, and from never realising how much they do and how much we demand.

Help us all through this day to try to do to others what we would wish them to do to us, and so help us to fulfil the law of Jesus Christ. This we ask for Thy love's sake. AMEN.

In the Evening

O God, our Father, this night we thank Thee for the comfort and the companionship and the love of this our home.

We thank Thee for the joy of being together in a family. We thank Thee for this day's work, and for this night's rest.

We ask Thee to bless those for whom there will be no sleep tonight; those who must work throughout the night; those who journey through the night by sea or land or air, to bring us our food, our letters, and our newspapers for the morning; those who must be on duty all night to maintain the public services, and to ensure the safety and the security of others; doctors who must wake to usher new life into the world, to close the eyes of those for whom this life is passing away, to ease the sufferer's pain; nurses and all who watch by the bedside of those who are ill; those who this night will not sleep because of the pain of their body or the distress of their mind; those in misfortune, who will lie down in hunger and in cold.

Grant that in our own happiness and our own comfort we may never forget the sorrow and the pain, the loneliness and the need of others in the slow, dark hours. This we ask for Thy love's sake.   AMEN.

Daily Reading

ISAIAH 53: 3–6

HE IS despised and rejected of men; a man of sorrows, and acquainted with grief: and we hid as it were our faces from him; he was despised, and we esteemed him not. Surely he hath borne our griefs, and carried our sorrows: yet we did esteem him stricken, smitten of God, and afflicted. But he was wounded for our transgressions, he was bruised for our iniquities: the chastisement of our peace was upon him; and with his stripes we are healed. All we like sheep have gone astray; we have turned every one to his own way; and the Lord hath laid on him the iniquity of us all.

In the Morning

O God, our Father, grant unto us all through this day patience with things and patience with people.

If any task will be difficult, grant us the perseverance which will not admit defeat.

If any problem will be hard to solve, help us not to abandon it, until we have found the solution.

If things will not come right the first time, help us to try and to try again, until failure becomes success.

Help us all through today never to lose our temper with people, however unfair, unjust, annoying and unpleasant they may be.

Help us to have time to listen to anyone who wants to talk to us about a worry, a problem, or a need.

Help us to be patient with those who are slow to learn and slow to understand.

Help us all through this day to work as Jesus worked, and to love as Jesus loved. This we ask for Thy love's sake. AMEN.

In the Evening

O God, our Father : as we look back across this day, we ask Thee to forgive us if today we have made things harder for others.

Forgive us if we have made work harder for others, by being careless, thoughtless, selfish and inconsiderate.

Forgive us if we have made faith harder for others, by laughing at things they hold precious, or casting doubts on things they hold dear.

Forgive us if we have made goodness harder for others, by setting them an example which would make it easier for them to go wrong.

Forgive us if we have made joy harder for others, by bringing gloom and depression through our grumbling discontent.

Forgive us, O God, for all the ugliness of our lives; and tomorrow help us to walk more nearly as our Master walked, that something of His grace and beauty may be on us. This we ask for Thy love's sake. AMEN.

Daily Reading

ROMANS 8: 35–39

WHO SHALL separate us from the love of Christ? shall tribulation, or distress, or persecution, of famine, or nakedness, or peril, or sword? As it is written, For thy sake we are killed all the day long; we are accounted as sheep for the slaughter. Nay, in all these things we are more than conquerors through him that loved us. For I am persuaded, that neither death, nor life, nor angels, nor principalities, nor powers, nor things present, nor things to come, nor height, nor depth, nor any other creature, shall be able to separate us from the love of God, which is in Christ Jesus our Lord.

In the Morning

O Lord our God, in whom we live and move and have our being, help us never to forget that Thou art beside us all through this day.
O Lord Jesus, who hast promised that Thou art with us always, help us never to forget Thy presence all this day.

So grant that all this day every word we speak may be fit for Thee to hear; that every deed we do may be fit for Thee to see; that even every thought of our mind and every emotion of our heart may be fit to bear Thy scrutiny.

Grant that every task we do may be so well done that we can take it and show it to Thee.
Grant that every pleasure in which we share may be so honourable and so clean that we can ask Thee to share it with us.

So bring us to the evening time with nothing left undone, and nothing badly done; with nothing to regret and nothing to make us ashamed: through Jesus Christ our Lord. AMEN.

In the Evening

O God, our Father, Master of all good workmen, always at evening time we remember the things which we have left undone.

Forgive us for the plans we made and did not carry out.
Forgive us for the resolutions we took and did not keep.

Forgive us for the promises we made and broke.
Forgive us for the tasks we began and never finished.

Grant that we may never put off a task or delay a decision until tomorrow, when it should be done and taken today. So help us to live that, whenever Thy call comes for us, at morning, at midday, or at evening, it may find us ready.

Now grant unto us this night the sleep which will bring rest to our bodies and peace to our minds; and grant that we may rise tomorrow to be better workmen and better servants of our Lord. This we ask for Thy love's sake.   AMEN.

Daily Reading

PSALM 95: 1-7

O COME, let us sing unto the Lord: let us make a joyful noise to the rock of our salvation

Let us come before his presence with thanksgiving, and make a joyful noise unto him with psalms.

For the Lord is a great God, and a great King above all gods.

In his hand are the deep places of the earth: the strength of the hills is his also.

The sea is his, and he made it: and his hands formed the dry land.

O come, let us worship and bow down: let us kneel before the Lord our maker.

For he is our God; and we are the people of his pasture, and the sheep of his hand.

In the Morning

Eternal God, who hast given unto us the gift of this another day, help us to use wisely and to use well the time which Thou hast given unto us.

Help us not to waste time on the wrong things, and on the things which do not matter.

Help us not to spend time in idleness, so that the hours go back to Thee unused and useless.

Help us not to put off until tomorrow that which should be done today, and ever to remember that we cannot tell if for us tomorrow will ever come.

Help us to do with our might each thing which our hand finds to do, and to do it as unto Thee, that we may come to the evening time with nothing left undone, and nothing badly done: through Jesus Christ our Lord.   AMEN.

In the Evening

O God, our Father, we thank Thee for all happy things which came to us this day.

We thank Thee for any kindness which we have received.

We thank Thee for any word of thanks or praise or encouragement which has come to us.

We thank Thee for anything which made us feel that we were needed and valued and appreciated.

We thank Thee for any new friendship that we have made, and for any old friendship which has become still more strong and precious.

We thank Thee for any temptation which we have been enabled to resist, and for any service that we have been enabled to render.

Accept, O God, all in this day which has been in accordance with Thy will, and forgive that which has not been so; and help us to lay ourselves to sleep in perfect fellowship with Thee and with our fellow-men: through Jesus Christ our Lord.   AMEN.

Daily Reading
EPHESIANS 6: 11–18

PUT ON the whole armour of God, that ye may be able to stand against the wiles of the devil. For we wrestle not against flesh and blood, but against principalities, against powers, against the rulers of the darkness of this world, against spiritual wickedness in high places. Wherefore take unto you the whole armour of God, that ye may be able to withstand the evil day, and having done all, to stand. Stand therefore, having your loins girt about with truth, and having on the breastplate of righteousness; and your feet shod with the preparation of the gospel of peace; above all taking the shield of faith, wherewith ye shall be able to quench all the fiery darts of the wicked. And take the helmet of salvation, and the sword of the Spirit, which is the word of God: praying always with all prayer and supplication in the Spirit, and watching thereunto with all perseverance and supplication for all saints.

In the Morning

O God, our Father, save us from these thoughts and feelings which only succeed in making life wretched and unhappy for ourselves and for others.

Save us from foolish discontent, and help us at all times to do the best we can with the resources we have.

Save us from the envy which forgets to count its own blessings, because it thinks so much of those of others.

Save us from the jealousy which grudges others every gift and every success.

Save us from vain regrets about things which cannot be altered; and give us grace to accept the situation in which we are, and there to serve Thee with our whole heart.

Save us from the bitterness which poisons life for ourselves and for others.

So grant that, cleansed from self and cleansed from sin, our lives may bring joy to others and contentment to ourselves: through Jesus Christ our Lord.   AMEN.

In the Evening

O God, our Father, bless those who at the day's ending specially need Thy blessing.

Bless those who are far from home and far from friends, and who are lonely as the shadows fall.

Bless those who have made mistakes and who are sorry now.

Bless those who are sad, and for whom loneliness is most lonely at evening time.

Bless those who are in illness and in pain, and for whom the night is slow and long.

Bless the people with whom we work every day.

Bless all our friends, and keep them true to us, and us true to them.

Bless our loved ones, and let nothing ever come between us and them.

Bless this family, and grant that it may be true of this home that, where two or three are gathered together Thou art there in the midst of them.

Bless each one of us. Thou knowest our needs better than we know them ourselves. Open Thou Thine hand and satisfy them all: through Jesus Christ our Lord. AMEN.

Daily Reading

PSALM 119: 97–104

O HOW love I thy law! it is my meditation all the day.

Thou through thy commandments hast made me wiser than mine enemies: for they are ever with me.

I have more understanding than all my teachers: for thy testimonies are my meditation.

I understand more than the ancients, because I keep thy precepts.

I have refrained my feet from every evil way, that I might keep thy word.

I have not departed from thy judgments: for thou hast taught me.

How sweet are thy words unto my taste! yea, sweeter than honey to my mouth!

Through thy precepts I get understanding: therefore I hate every false way.

In the Morning

Eternal God, grant that we may count it a day wasted when we do not learn something new, and when we are not a little further on on the way to goodness and to Thee.

Help us to try to do our work better every day.

Help us to try to add something to our store of knowledge every day.

Help us to try to know some one better every day.

Grant unto us each day to learn more of self-mastery and self control.

Grant unto us each day better to rule our temper and our tongue.

Grant unto us each day to leave our faults farther behind and to grow more nearly into the likeness of our Lord.

So grant that at the end of this day, and at the end of every day, we may be nearer to Thee than when the day began : through Jesus Christ our Lord.

AMEN.

In the Evening

O God, our Father, forgive us for the failures of today.

Forgive us for any failure in self-control, through which we said or did things for which we are sorry now.

Forgive us for any failure in self-discipline, through which we were slack, when we should have been doing with our might that which our hand found to do.

Forgive us for any failure in obedience, through which we listened to our own desires rather than to Thy will.

We give Thee thanks for anything of good that has been in this day.

We thank Thee for any temptation which Thou didst enable us to overcome.

We thank Thee for any help Thou didst enable us to give, and for any service Thou didst enable us to render.

We thank Thee for any good word which Thou didst enable us to speak, and any good deed which Thou didst enable us to do.

So now we render this day back to Thee, with all its dark times and all its shining moments, that Thou mayest accept its goodness and forgive its sin : through Jesus Christ our Lord.   AMEN.

Daily Reading

MATTHEW 20 : 25–28

JESUS CALLED them unto him, and said, Ye know that the princes of the Gentiles exercise dominion over them, and they that are great exercise authority upon them. But it shall be so among you : but whosoever will be great among you, let him be your minister ; and whosoever will be chief among you, let him be your servant : even as the Son of man came not to be ministered unto, but to minister, and to give his life a ransom for many.

In the Morning

O God, our Father, we are ashamed when we remember how so often we hurt most of all those whom we ought to cherish most of all, and how we treat our nearest and dearest in a way in which we would never dare to behave towards strangers. Grant that it may not be so today.

Take from us the carelessness, the selfishness, the inconsiderateness, the untidiness, which make the work of others harder than it ought to be.

Take from us the lack of sensitiveness, which makes us hurt the feelings of others, and never even realise that we are doing so.

Take from us the habit of unkind criticism and of nagging fault-finding, the temper of crossness and irritability, which wreck the peace of any home.

Take from us the disobedience, which brings anxiety, and the disloyalty which brings sorrow to those who love us.

Grant that all through today we may so speak and so act that we will bring nothing but happiness to those whose love is our privilege, and whose friendship is our joy : through Jesus Christ our Lord.   AMEN.

In the Evening

O God, our Father, we thank Thee for everything which has happened to us today, because we know that in it and through it all Thou hast been loving us with an everlasting love.

We thank Thee alike for sorrow and for joy, for laughter and for tears, for silence and for song.

We thank Thee for any success to lift life up, and for any failure to keep us humble and to help us not to forget our need of Thee.

We thank Thee for joys which will be to us for ever and for ever happy memories, and we thank Thee for sorrows which made us go to Thee because we had nowhere else to go.

Grant unto us at all times, no matter what is happening to us, the certainty that Thou art working all things together for good. And so grant that this night our pillow may be peace : through Jesus Christ our Lord.

AMEN.

Daily Reading

PSALM 103 : 8–13

THE LORD is merciful and gracious, slow to anger, and plenteous in mercy. He will not always chide : neither will he keep his anger for ever. He hath not dealt with us after our sins ; nor rewarded us according to our iniquities. For as the heaven is high above the earth, so great is his mercy toward them that fear him. As far as the east is from the west, so far hath he removed our transgressions from us. Like as a father pitieth his children, so the Lord pitieth them that fear him.

In the Morning

O God, our Father, help us to walk with wisdom all this day.

Help us never to flirt with temptation, and never to play with fire.

Help us never needlessly or thoughtlessly to put ourselves into a position in which temptation has the opportunity to exert its power over us.

Help us never to allow our eyes to linger, or our thoughts to dwell, on the forbidden things, lest their fascination be too strong for our resistance.

Help us to walk every step of today looking ever unto Jesus, that His light may be our guide, that His presence may be our defence, and that His love may be our strength and inspiration. This we ask for Thy love's sake. AMEN.

In the Evening

O God, our Father, giver of every good and perfect gift, put into our hearts gratitude for all that Thou hast done for us today.

Help us not to forget that today Thou hast kept us in our going out and our coming in, and hast brought us to this evening hour; that today Thou hast fed us and clothed us and given us life and kept us alive; that today Thou hast preserved us in body, mind and spirit, and hast surrounded us with love both human and divine.

O God, our Father, who dost ever accept the offering of the humble and the contrite heart, put into our hearts penitence for all the failures, the faults, the mistakes, the sins of this day. Make us to see ourselves and our sins in the light of Thy pure countenance. So make us truly sorry for every wrong thing which has shamed ourselves and grieved Thee, and then grant us, before we sleep, Thy kiss of pardon and of peace: through Jesus Christ our Lord. AMEN.

Daily Reading

LUKE 15: 3–10

AND HE spake this parable unto them, saying, What man of you, having an hundred sheep, if he lose one of them, doth not leave the ninety and nine in the wilderness, and go after that which is lost, until he find it? And when he hath found it, he layeth it on his shoulders, rejoicing. And when he cometh home, he calleth together his friends and neighbours, saying unto them, Rejoice with me; for I have found my sheep which was lost. I say unto you, that likewise joy shall be in heaven over one sinner that repenteth, more than over ninety and nine just persons, which need no repentance. Either what woman having ten pieces of silver, if she lose one piece, doth not light a candle, and sweep the house, and seek diligently till she find it? And when she hath found it, she calleth her friends and her neighbours together, saying, Rejoice with me; for I have found the piece which I had lost. Likewise, I say unto you, there is joy in the presence of the angels of God over one sinner that repenteth.

In the Morning

O God, our Father, we know that every day comes to us from Thee filled with new opportunities; and we know that today will be like that.

We know that today will bring us the opportunity to do some useful work, and to justify our existence in the world; help us to do that work with all our might.

We know that today will bring us the opportunity to learn something new, and to add something to the store of our knowledge; help us to seize that opportunity.

We know that today will bring us the opportunity to witness for Thee, and to show on whose side we are; help us fearlessly to bear that witness.

We know that today will bring us an opportunity to lend a helping hand to those whose need is greater than our own; help us to be among our fellowmen as they who serve.

We know that today will bring us the opportunity to come closer to each other and nearer to Thee; grant that we may so take that opportunity that, when the evening comes, we may be bound more firmly in comradeship to one another, and in love to Thee: through Jesus Christ our Lord.   AMEN.

In the Evening

O God, our Father, forgive us if we have been too lazy today.

Forgive us if we have left undone tasks which should have been done; if we have left untaken decisions which should have been taken; if we have not kept the promises we should have kept.

O God, our Father, forgive us if we have allowed ourselves to be too busy today.

Forgive us if we have been too busy to help a friend, even if it was only by patiently listening to his troubles; if we have been too busy to fulfil our duties to our family and to our home. Forgive us if moment has added itself to moment, and hour to hour, and we were too busy to think of Thee.

Grant unto us this night to sleep well, and, on the morrow, grant unto us to wake and to work without haste and without rest, so that, like our Master, we may finish the work which Thou hast given us to do. This we ask for Thy love's sake.   AMEN.

Daily Reading

PSALM 19: 7–11

THE LAW of the Lord is perfect, converting the soul: the testimony of the Lord is sure, making wise the simple.

The statutes of the Lord are right, rejoicing the heart: the commandment of the Lord is pure, enlightening the eyes.

The fear of the Lord is clean, enduring for ever: the judgments of the Lord are true and righteous altogether.

More to be desired are they than gold, yea, than much fine gold: sweeter also than honey and the honeycomb.

Moreover by them is thy servant warned: and in keeping of them there is great reward.

In the Morning

O God, our Father, deliver us this day from all that would keep us from serving Thee and from serving our fellowmen as we ought.

Deliver us from all coldness of heart; and grant that neither our hand nor our heart may ever remain shut to the appeal of someone's need.

Deliver us from all weakness of will; from the indecision which cannot make up its mind; from the irresolution which cannot abide by a decision once it is made; from the inability to say No to the tempting voices which come to us from inside and from outside.

Deliver us from all failure in endeavour; from being too easily discouraged; from giving up and giving in too soon; from allowing any task to defeat us, because it is difficult.

Grant unto us this day the love which is generous in help; the determination which is steadfast in decision; the perseverance which is enduring unto the end; through Jesus Christ our Lord. AMEN.

In the Evening

O God, our Father, take from our minds this night the worries and anxieties which would keep us from sleeping. Help us to make up our minds bravely to deal with the things which can be dealt with, and not to worry about the things about which we can do nothing.

Take from our hearts this night the feelings which would keep us from resting; take from us all discontent, all envy and jealousy, all vain and useless longings for the things which are not for us.

Take from our bodies the tension which would keep us from relaxing; and help us to lean back in the clasp of the everlasting arms.

Into Thy hands we commit our loved ones, knowing that, even if they are absent from us, they are for ever present with Thee. Into Thy hands we commit ourselves that in Thy keeping, in light and in dark, in life and in death, we may be safe.

Hear these our prayers, through Jesus Christ our Lord.

AMEN.

Daily Reading

MARK 10: 13–16

AND THEY brought young children to him, that he should touch them: and his disciples rebuked those that brought them. But when Jesus saw it, he was much displeased, and said unto them, Suffer the little children to come unto me, and forbid them not: for of such is the kingdom of God. Verily I say unto you, Whosoever shall not receive the kingdom of God as a little child, he shall not enter therein. And he took them up in his arms, put his hands upon them, and blessed them.

In the Morning

O God, our Father, who hast given unto us the rest of the night, and who dost now send us forth to the work of the day, guide us and direct us all through today.

Help us to work aright, so that every task may be so well done that we can take it and show it unto Thee.

Help us to speak aright, and preserve us alike from too hasty speech and from cowardly silence.

Help us to think aright, and so guard our minds and hearts that no evil and no bitter thought may gain an entry in to them.

Help us to live as befits those who have begun this day with Thee, and who go out to live every moment of it in Thy presence. Grant that today our lives may shine like lights of love and goodness in the world, that we may bring credit to the name we bear, and honour to the Master, whose we are and whom we seek to serve. This we ask for Thy love's sake.

AMEN.

In the Evening

O God, our Father, we thank Thee for today.

We thank Thee that Thou hast given us strength and health of body and of mind to do our work and to earn a living.

We thank Thee for our loved ones, and for all our comrades and our friends, without whom life could never be the same.

O God, our Father, grant us Thy forgiveness for today.

Forgive us if today our work was badly done, no better than our second best.

Forgive us if today we failed a friend, or hurt and disappointed anyone who loves us.

And now, as we go to rest, grant us the peace of those who have cast all their burdens upon Thee, and who know that their times are always in Thy hand. This we ask for Thy love's sake.   AMEN.

Daily Reading

PSALM 116: 1-8

I LOVE the Lord, because he hath heard my voice and my supplications.

Because he hath inclined his ear unto me, therefore will I call upon him as long as I live.

The sorrows of death compassed me, and the pains of hell gat hold upon me : I found trouble and sorrow.

Then called I upon the name of the Lord ; O Lord, I beseech thee, deliver my soul.

Gracious is the Lord, and righteous ; yea, our God is merciful.

The Lord preserveth the simple : I was brought low, and he helped me.

Return unto thy rest, O my soul ; for the Lord hath dealt bountifully with thee.

For thou hast delivered my soul from death, mine eyes from tears, and my feet from falling.

In the Morning

O God, our Father, grant that whatever happens to us today we may take it to Thee.

If we shall have decisions to make, help us to ask Thy guidance, and grant us humility and obedience to take it when Thou dost give it to us.

If we shall have problems to solve, help us to ask Thy light upon them, so that we may see a clear way through them.

If we shall have hard and difficult things to do, help us to ask for Thy strength, so that we may be enabled to do the things which we could not do ourselves.

If we shall have temptations to face, help us to seek Thy grace, remembering that Jesus, because He was tempted, is able to help others who are tempted.

Help us all through today to decide everything by Thy will, and to test everything by Thy presence, so that we may come to the day's ending without mistakes and without regrets : through Jesus Christ our Lord.

AMEN.

In the Evening

O God, our Father, we give Thee thanks for every part of the day which is coming to an end.

We thank Thee for the morning light to call us from our resting beds.

We thank Thee for the midday hours filled with work and with many activities in the company of our fellow-men.

We thank Thee for the evening time to sit at home amidst our family circle, or to go out upon our pleasures with our friends. And now we thank Thee for the night and for kindly sleep.

We thank Thee for every happy thing which has come to us this day, and for all things which bring us joy when we remember them.

We ask Thy forgiveness for everything in today which hurts us and shames us when we remember it.

Grant unto us now to lay ourselves down, and to sleep in peace, because we are at peace with Thee, and at peace with our fellow-men: through Jesus Christ our Lord. AMEN.

Daily Reading

PHILIPPIANS 4: 4–8

REJOICE IN the Lord alway: and again I say, Rejoice Let your moderation be known unto all men. The Lord is at hand. Be careful for nothing; but in everything by prayer and supplication with thanksgiving let your requests be made known unto God. And the peace of God, which passeth all understanding, shall keep your hearts and minds through Christ Jesus. Finally, brethren, whatsoever things are true, whatsoever things are honest, whatsoever things are just, whatsoever things are pure, whatsoever things are lovely, whatsoever things are of good report; if there be any virtue, and if there be any praise, think on these things.

TWENTY-SECOND DAY

In the Morning

O God, our Father, help us this day to treat all men aright.

Help us to be a good example to those who are younger than we are; to be respectful to those who are older than we are; and to be at all times courteous to our equals.

Help us to be obedient to those who are set in authority over us; and to be just and fair and kind to any over whom we have control.

Help us to be sympathetic to those in distress, to be helpful to those in trouble, and to be kind to those in need.

So make us all this day to go about doing good as our Master did. This we ask for Thy love's sake.

AMEN.

In the Evening

O God, our Father, if we have hurt anyone today, give us grace to say that we are sorry.

If we have been wrong in anything today, give us grace to admit our error.

If we have been resentful today, help us in the time to come to accept rebuke in the spirit of humility, even if we think that we do not deserve it.

If we have parted with anyone in anger today, or if there has been a misunderstanding between us and anyone else, give us grace to take the first step to put things right.

If we have been unjust or unfair, or, if we have said things in the heat of the moment which we would not have said if we had stopped to think, give us grace to apologize.

Help us this night, before we lay ourselves to sleep, to make up our minds that we will leave no breach between us and anyone else unhealed. This we ask for Thy love's sake.   AMEN.

Daily Reading

JOSHUA I : 6–9

BE STRONG and of good courage : for unto this people shalt thou divide for an inheritance the land, which I sware unto their fathers to give them.   Only be thou strong and very courageous, that thou mayest observe to do according to all the law, which Moses my servant commanded thee : turn not from it to the right hand or to the left, that thou mayest prosper whithersoever thou goest.   This book of the law shall not depart out of thy mouth ; but thou shalt meditate therein day and night, that thou mayest observe to do according to all that is written therein : for then thou shalt make thy way prosperous, and then thou shalt have good success. Have not I commanded thee ?   Be strong and of a good courage ; be not afraid, neither be thou dismayed : for the Lord thy God is with thee whithersoever thou goest.

In the Morning

O God, our Father, help us this day to work faithfully and to work well.

Grant that we may put off until tomorrow no task which should be done today.

Grant that we may not do with a grudge that which should be done with a smile.

Grant that we may never be content to render to anyone else that which is less than our best.

Help us all through this day to be as kind to others as we would wish them to be with us.

Help us always to be honest, never to be guilty of any mean action or any sharp practice, and never to seek an unfair advantage over others.

Help us all through this day to work in such a way that when the evening comes we shall hear Thee say: " Well done ! "

Hear this our prayer for Thy love's sake.   AMEN.

In the Evening

O God, our Father, be with us as this day ends.

If we are feeling depressed, if we have honestly done our best and yet feel that we are a failure, help us to know that Thou dost understand.

If we are well aware that we have done something wrong today, save us from the foolishness of trying to hide it from Thee; and help us to tell Thee about it, knowing that, if we are truly sorry, Thou wilt forgive.

If things have hurt us today, if people have been unkind and friends have been unfaithful, help us to remember that Jesus too knows what it is like, because He went through it.

If today has been a happy day, and life has been sweet, help us not to forget now to give Thee thanks.

Before we sleep, we give Thee thanks for all Thy goodness; we ask Thy pardon for all our sins and our mistakes; and we ask Thy blessing on ourselves and on those we love: through Jesus Christ our Lord.

AMEN.

Daily Reading

MATTHEW 7: 7-12

ASK, AND it shall be given you; seek, and ye shall find; knock, and it shall be opened unto you: for every one that asketh receiveth; and he that seeketh findeth; and to him that knocketh it shall be opened. Or what man is there of you, whom if his son ask bread, will he give him a stone? Or if he ask a fish, will he give him a serpent? If ye then, being evil, know how to give good gifts unto your children, how much more shall your Father which is in heaven give good things to them that ask him? Therefore all things whatsoever ye would that men should do to you, do ye even so to them: for this is the law and the prophets.

In the Morning

O God, our Father, who hast made all things and made them well, we thank Thee for sleep by night and for work by day.

We thank Thee for this world which Thou hast made; for night and day; for light and dark; for sunset and for dawn.

We thank Thee that Thou hast made us as we are. We thank Thee for hands to work and feet to walk; for eyes to see and ears to hear; for minds to think and plan, for memories to remember, and for hearts to love.

We thank Thee for those who today will teach us, for those to whom we will go for advice, and for those on whose wisdom and experience we will draw to help us to do our work, and to solve our problems.

We thank Thee for those whose friendship every day gives strength and whose love gives glory to our lives.

Above all else we thank Thee for Jesus Christ, our blessed Lord. Grant that all through today we may never forget His presence always with us. This we ask for Thy love's sake.   AMEN.

In the Evening

O God, our Father, we remember before Thee those who dread and fear the night.

Bless those in pain and in distress of body; those who, although they are tired, cannot sleep; those whom worry has robbed of rest; those for whom the world seems very empty and very lonely at evening time; little children who are lonely and afraid of the dark.

Forgive us this night for all the wrong that we have this day done, even for the things for which we find it hard to forgive ourselves.

Grant us this night the mind at rest in the peace that passeth understanding; the heart content in the love from which nothing can separate us; and the life which is hid with Christ in Thee.

This we ask for Thy love's sake.   AMEN.

Daily Reading

PSALM 139: 7-14

WHITHER SHALL I go from thy spirit? or whither shall I flee from thy presence?

If I ascend up into heaven, thou art there: if I make my bed in hell, behold, thou art there.

If I take the wings of the morning, and dwell in the uttermost parts of the sea;

Even there shall thy hand lead me, and thy right hand shall hold me.

If I say, Surely the darkness shall cover me; even the night shall be light about me.

Yea, the darkness hideth not from thee; but the night shineth as the day: the darkness and the light are both alike to thee.

For thou hast possessed my reins: thou hast covered me in my mother's womb.

I will praise thee; for I am fearfully and wonderfully made: marvellous are thy works; and that my soul knoweth right well.

In the Morning

O God, our Father, whose love is over every creature whom Thine hands have made, as we go out this morning to the world and our work we ask Thee to bless all classes and conditions of men and women everywhere.

Bless those who are servants, and help them to serve with diligence; and bless those who are masters, and help them to direct and to control with justice and with mercy.

Bless those who are rich, and help them to remember that they must hold all their possessions in stewardship for Thee; and bless those who are poor, and grant that they may find others kind.

Bless those who are strong and fit, and grant that they may never use their good health selfishly; and bless those who are weak and ailing, and keep them from all discouragement and discontent.

Bless those who are happy, and help them not to forget Thee in the sunny weather; and bless those who are sad, and ease the pain and comfort the loneliness of their hearts.

Bless the animals who are the friends and the servants of men, and grant that none may treat them with cruelty, but that all may be kind to them.

Bless each one of us, and grant that we may go out to live as those who have been with Jesus. This we ask for Thy love's sake. AMEN.

In the Evening

O God, our Father, who art plenteous in mercy, forgive us for all the wrong things which have spoiled today.

Forgive us for any moment when the voice of conscience spoke to us, and we heard it, but went our own way.

Forgive us for any moment when we forgot Thee; when we were so immersed in the affairs and the pleasures of this world that we had no thought to spare for Thee.

Forgive us for any moment when we grieved Thee; for any word or action or conduct which made men think less of the name we bear.

Forgive us if today we have neglected duty, failed in witness, wavered in faith, fallen away from love.

When we think of our own failure we thank Thee most of all for Jesus Christ, who gave His life a ransom for many, and who is the Lamb of God who taketh away the sin of the world, and our sin. Grant that before we sleep we may find in Him Thy pardon and Thy peace. This we ask for Thy love's sake. AMEN.

Daily Reading

MATTHEW 7: 16–20

Ye shall know them by their fruits. Do men gather grapes of thorns, or figs of thistles? Even so every good tree bringeth forth good fruit; but a corrupt tree bringeth forth evil fruit. A good tree cannot bring forth evil fruit, neither can a corrupt tree bring forth good fruit. Every tree that bringeth not forth good fruit is hewn down, and cast into the fire. Wherefore by their fruits ye shall know them.

In the Morning

O God, our Father, grant us Thy blessing as we go out to meet this day.

Grant unto us this day lips which speak the truth, but which ever speak the truth in love.

Grant unto us minds which seek the truth; and grant that we may face the truth even when it hurts and condemns us, and that we may never shut our eyes to that which we do not wish to see.

Grant unto us hands which work with diligence, and which yet have time to help another with his task.

Grant unto us resolution to stand for principle; but save us from stubbornness, and from magnifying trifles into principles.

Grant unto us grace to conquer our temptations and to live in purity; but save us from the self-righteousness which would look down on anyone who has fallen by the way.

All through this day grant unto us the strength and the gentleness of our blessed Lord. This we ask for Thy love's sake. AMEN.

In the Evening

O God, our Father, there are things in today which make us ashamed when we remember them.

Forgive us if we have lost our temper with the people who get on our nerves.

Forgive us if we have been cross and irritable with those who are nearest and dearest to us.

Forgive us if at any time we were discourteous and

impolite to those with whom we came in contact in our work.

Forgive us if we have thoughtlessly or deliberately hurt anyone's feelings today.

O God, our Father, there are things in today which make us glad when we remember them.

We thank Thee for any lovely thing that we have seen, for any wise thing that we have heard, and for any good thing that we have been enabled to do.

We thank Thee for the time we have spent with our friends and comrades, and with those we love.

O God, our Father, accept our sorrow for our sins and our gratitude for Thy gifts before we sleep this night: through Jesus Christ our Lord.   AMEN.

Daily Reading

ISAIAH 2: 2-4

AND IT shall come to pass in the last days, that the mountain of the Lord's house shall be established in the top of the mountains, and shall be exalted above the hills; and all nations shall flow unto it. And many people shall go and say, Come ye, and let us go up to the mountain of the Lord, to the house of the God of Jacob; and he will teach us of his ways, and we will walk in his paths: for out of Zion shall go forth the law, and the word of the Lord from Jerusalem. And he shall judge among the nations, and shall rebuke many people: and they shall beat their swords into plowshares, and their spears into pruninghooks: nation shall not lift up sword against nation, neither shall they learn war any more.

In the Morning

O God, our Father, help us all through this day to obey Thy law, and to do unto others all that we would wish them to do unto us.

Grant unto us to help others, as we would wish them to help us, when we are in difficulty or in distress.

Help us to forgive others as we would wish them to forgive us, when we make mistakes.

Help us to make the same allowances for others as we would wish them to make for us.

Help us to have the same sympathy for others as we would wish them to have for us, when we are sad.

Help us to have the same respect and tolerance for the views and for the beliefs of others as we would wish them to have for ours.

Help us to try to understand others as we would wish to be understood.

Help us so to enter into others that we may see things with their eyes, and think things with their minds, and feel things with their hearts; and so grant that we may be as kind to others as we would wish them to be to us: through Jesus Christ our Lord.   AMEN.

In the Evening

O God, our Father, bless those for whom life is unhappy.

Bless those who are underpaid and overworked, those who never have enough, and who are always tired.

Bless those who are always taken for granted, and who are never thanked, and praised, and appreciated, as they ought to be.

Bless those who have been hurt by life, those who have been wounded by the malice of their enemies, or by the faithlessness of their friends.

Bless those who have been disappointed in something on which they had set their hearts.

Bless those for whom life is lonely and empty, because some one they loved has been taken away.

Bless those whom illness or weakness has handicapped or laid aside.

Bless those who are worried about those they love.

Thou knowest the needs of each one of us, and Thou knowest the secrets of our inmost hearts. Help us this night to cast all our burdens upon Thee, certain that Thou carest for us, and sure that Thou wilt help. This we ask for Thy love's sake. AMEN.

Daily Reading

JOHN 3: 14–17

AND AS Moses lifted up the serpent in the wilderness, even so must the Son of man be lifted up : that whosoever believeth in him should not perish, but have eternal life. For God so loved the world, that he gave his only begotten Son, that whosoever believeth in him should not perish, but have everlasting life. For God sent not his Son into the world to condemn the world ; but that the world through him might be saved.

In the Morning

O God, our Father, grant unto us all through this day to do not what we like but what we ought. Grant unto us all through this day to follow Thy will and not our own desires.

Help us to do with diligence the tasks we do not wish to do.

Help us to meet with graciousness the people we do not like to meet.

Help us in all things to set duty above pleasure.

Grant that conscience may be our only master, and that our only motive may be to do things well enough to take them and to show them unto Thee.

Grant unto us never to seek to do as little as possible and to get as much as possible; never to seek to evade our work; never to leave to others that which we ourselves should do; never to avoid the decisions we ought to make, or to shirk the responsibilities we ought to shoulder.

So grant that at the evening time we may know the deep contentment of work completed and of duty done: through Jesus Christ our Lord.   AMEN.

In the Evening

O God, our Father, forgive us for everything in this day which has grieved Thee to see.

Forgive us if we have made the work of others harder instead of easier.

Forgive us if we have discouraged others instead of encouraging them.

Forgive us if our presence has depressed others instead of making them happier.

Forgive us if we have grumbled and complained, and so made things unhappy for ourselves and for everyone else.

Forgive us if we have been cross, irritable, bad-tempered, fault-finding, and difficult to live with.

Forgive us if we have made it easier for some one else to do wrong, and harder for him to do right.

Forgive us if we have been ungracious and ungrateful.

Forgive us if we have worried our friends, or hurt our loved ones.

Forgive us for all the things of which we are now ashamed, and give us grace tomorrow to walk more close to Thee; through Jesus Christ our Lord.   AMEN.

Daily Reading

PSALM 24: 1-5

THE EARTH is the Lord's, and the fulness thereof; the world, and they that dwell therein.

For he hath founded it upon the seas, and established it upon the floods.

Who shall ascend into the hill of the Lord? or who shall stand in his holy place?

He that hath clean hands, and a pure heart; who hath not lifted up his soul unto vanity, nor sworn deceitfully.

He shall receive the blessing from the Lord, and righteousness from the God of his salvation.

In the Morning

O God, our Father, help us to learn the lessons that life is seeking to teach us.

Save us from making the same mistakes over and over again.

Save us from falling to the same temptations time and time again.

Save us from doing things that we should not do, until the doing of them has become a habit which we cannot break.

Save us from failing to realize our own weaknesses, and from refusing to see our own faults.

Save us from persisting in courses of action which we ought to have learned long ago can lead to nothing but trouble.

Save us from doing things which we know annoy other people.

Help us daily to grow stronger, purer, kinder.

Help us daily to shed old faults, and to gain new virtues, until, by Thy grace, life becomes altogether new.

Hear this our morning prayer for Thy love's sake.

AMEN.

In the Evening

O God, our Father, we thank Thee for this day.

We thank Thee for those who have given us guidance, counsel, advice and good example.

We thank Thee for those in whose company the sun shone even in the rain, and who brought a smile to our faces even when things were grim.

We thank Thee for those in whose company the frightening things were not so alarming, and the hard things not so difficult.

We thank Thee for those whose presence saved us from falling to temptation, and enabled us to do the right.

We thank Thee for those whom it is joy even to be with, and in whose company the hours pass all too quickly.

We thank Thee for happy times to be to us for ever happy memories.

We thank Thee for times of failure to keep us humble, and to make us remember how much we need Thee.

Most of all we thank Thee for Jesus Christ, who in the daytime is our friend and our companion and who in the night is our pillow and our peace.

Hear this our evening thanksgiving for Thy love's sake.

AMEN.

Daily Reading

ROMANS 12 : 10–16

BE KINDLY affectioned one to another with brotherly love; in honour preferring one another; not slothful in business; fervent in spirit; serving the Lord; rejoicing in hope; patient in tribulation; continuing instant in prayer; distributing to the necessity of saints; given to hospitality. Bless them which persecute you: bless, and curse not. Rejoice with them that do rejoice, and weep with them that weep. Be of the same mind one toward another. Mind not high things, but condescend to men of low estate. Be not wise in your own conceits.

___

In the Morning

O God, our Father, equip us with these gifts of Thine which will enable us to live aright today and every day.

Grant unto us the faith which can accept the things which it cannot understand, and which will never turn to doubt.

Grant unto us the hope which still hopes on, even in the dark, and which will never turn to despair.

Grant unto us the loyalty which will be true to Thee, even though all men deny Thee, and which will never stoop to compromise.

Grant unto us the purity which can resist all the seductions of temptation, and which can never be turned from the straight way.

Arm our wills with Thy strength, and fill our hearts with Thy love, so that we may be strong to obey Thee and loving to serve our fellow-men, and so be like our Master. This we ask for Thy love's sake.   AMEN.

In the Evening

O God, our Father, we remember all the failures of today.

Forgive us for any promises we broke today, or any resolutions we failed to keep.

Forgive us for any friends we failed today, or any people we hurt.

Forgive us for any carelessness in our work today, or any neglect of duty.

Forgive us for any mean, ungenerous, or dishonourable deed today, for any false, impure, or angry word.

O God, our Father, we remember all who have helped us today.

We thank Thee for those who helped us with our work.
We thank Thee for those who helped us to resist our temptations.
We thank Thee for anyone who gave us a word of thanks, of encouragement, of praise, or of appreciation.
We thank Thee for those who sent us happier on our way, because we met them.

More than anything else we thank Thee for Jesus, our Saviour and our Friend.

Grant that we may show our penitence for our failures, and our gratitude for Thy gifts by waking to do better tomorrow, and to walk more closely with Thee. This we ask for Thy love's sake.   AMEN.

Daily Reading

ISAIAH I : 16–18

WASH YOU, make you clean ; put away the evil of your doings from before mine eyes ; cease to do evil ; learn to do well ; seek judgment, relieve the oppressed, judge the fatherless, plead for the widow. Come now, and let us reason together, saith the Lord : though your sins be as scarlet, they shall be as white as snow ; though they be red like crimson, they shall be as wool.

PRAYERS WITH BIBLE READINGS
FOR FOUR SUNDAYS

FIRST SUNDAY

In the Morning

O God, our Father, we give Thee thanks for this Lord's day. Help us to use it for Thy glory, and for our own good, as Thou wouldst have us to do.

Help us to use it to rest, so that tomorrow we may go back refreshed to our work.

Help us to use it in company with our friends and loved ones, that we may enter into even closer fellowship with them.

Help us to use it to worship Thee, to talk with Thee, to listen to Thee, to come ever closer to Thee, that we may go back to the days of the week never to forget Thee any more.

Bless those who will preach or teach Thy truth this day, in this land and in lands across the sea, and grant that for them a door of utterance may be opened; and so prosper Thy word, on the lips of Thy preachers and in the ears of Thy listeners, that it may not return unto Thee void and empty, but that it may accomplish that whereto Thou didst send it. This we ask for Thy love's sake. AMEN.

In the Evening

O God, our Father, whose desire it is that all men should be saved, bless every word which has been spoken in Thy name today; and grant that the words of Thy teachers and Thy preachers may have winged their way into the hidden depths of many a heart.

We ask Thee very specially to bless all missionaries, who have gone out to take Thy word to the distant places of the earth.

In their loneliness, cheer them; in their difficulties, strengthen them; in their problems, encourage them; in their tasks, inspire them. And grant that they may ever be upheld by the remembrance that we are thinking of them, and praying for them. Hasten the day when the knowledge of Thee shall cover the earth as the waters cover the sea.

Bless each one of us; and grant that it may not be for nothing that we have companied with Thee this day, but grant that the fruit of the Spirit may enrich our lives, because we worshipped Thee: through Jesus Christ our Lord. AMEN.

Daily Reading

LUKE 4: 16-19

AND JESUS came to Nazareth where he had been brought up: and, as his custom was, he went into the synagogue on the sabbath day, and stood up for to read. And there was delivered unto him the book of the prophet Esaias. And when he had opened the book, he found the place where it was written, The Spirit of the Lord is upon me, because he hath anointed me to preach the gospel to the poor; he hath sent me to heal the brokenhearted, to preach deliverance to the captives, and recovering of sight to the blind, to set at liberty them that are bruised, to preach the acceptable year of the Lord.

In the Morning

O God, our Father, we thank Thee for this Thine own day.

We thank Thee for this day's rest, in which we lay aside our daily work and tasks to relax our bodies, to refresh our minds, and to strengthen our spirits.

We thank Thee for this day's worship, in which we lay aside our cares and our anxieties to concentrate our every thought on Thee alone.

We thank Thee for Thy Church. We thank Thee for the fellowship we enjoy within it; for the teaching which is given to us; for the guidance for life and living which we receive.

We thank Thee for the reading of Thy word, for the preaching of Thy truth, for the singing of Thy praise, for the prayers of Thy people, and for the sacraments of Thy grace.

Grant that in this day of Thine we may receive such strength and guidance, that we shall be enabled to go out to walk with Thee, and not to fall from Thee, in all the days of this week which lies ahead: through Jesus Christ our Lord. AMEN.

In the Evening

O God, our Father, we thank Thee for this day to whose ending we are come.

We thank Thee for hours that we have spent within the four walls of this place which we call home.

We thank Thee for hours that we have spent in the fellowship of our comrades and our friends.

We thank Thee for hours that we have spent in the company of those we love.

We thank Thee for hours we have spent in the fellowship of Thy worshipping people in Thy Church.

We thank Thee for any truth that we have heard; for any guidance that we have received; and for any new tokens of Thy love which have been granted unto us.

Grant, O God, that, when tomorrow we go forth to the world's work and ways, we may use, to Thy glory, that which we have received by Thy grace: through Jesus Christ our Lord.   AMEN.

Daily Reading

PSALM 122

I WAS glad when they said unto me, Let us go into the house of the Lord.

Our feet shall stand within thy gates, O Jerusalem.

Jerusalem is builded as a city that is compact together:

Whither the tribes go up, the tribes of the Lord, unto the testimony of Israel, to give thanks unto the name of the Lord.

For there are set thrones of judgment, the thrones of the house of David

Pray for the peace of Jerusalem: they shall prosper that love thee.

Peace be within thy walls, and prosperity within thy palaces.

For my brethren and companions' sakes, I will now say, Peace be within thee.

Because of the house of the Lord our God I will seek thy good.

In the Morning

O God, our Father, we thank Thee for everything which brings us nearer to Thee.

We thank Thee for Thy book, to tell us of Thy dealings with Thy people, and to set before us the deeds and words of our blessed Lord in the days of His flesh.

We thank Thee for the music and the poetry of the psalms and the hymns we sing, and for all the memories which they awaken.

We thank Thee for the open door of prayer which no man can ever shut.

We thank Thee for this day with its call to lay aside the things of earth and to enter into Thy house.

We thank Thee for the preaching of Thy word, to comfort our hearts and to enlighten our minds.

We thank Thee for the sacraments of Thy grace to be the channels of the love divine.

Open our minds and hearts today, that in it and in its worship we may receive the precious things which Thou art waiting to give: through Jesus Christ our Lord.   AMEN.

In the Evening

O God, our Father, grant that at the ending of this day Thou mayest be nearer and dearer to us.

Send us back tomorrow to our duties and tasks with a greater knowledge in our minds, a greater love within our hearts, and a firmer grip upon Thine hand.

Help us not to forget the truth that we have learned today. Grant that the stirrings of our heart may not have been all to no purpose.

Help us to go out and to live that to which we have listened, and to practise that which we have professed.

Grant that we may come to the end of this day with the sense of sins forgiven, and with the cleansing power within us to enable us to live more nearly as we ought.

This day again we have remembered how Jesus Christ died for us; send us out tomorrow to live for Him: through Jesus Christ our Lord.   AMEN.

Daily Reading

MARK 2: 23–28

AND IT came to pass, that he went through the corn fields on the sabbath day; and his disciples began, as they went, to pluck the ears of corn. And the Pharisees said unto him, Behold, why do they on the sabbath day that which is not lawful? And he said unto them, Have ye never read what David did, when he had need, and was an hungred, he, and they that were with him? How he went into the house of God in the days of Abiathar the high priest, and did eat the shewbread, which is not lawful to eat but for the priests, and gave also to them which were with him? And he said unto them, The sabbath was made for man, and not man for the sabbath: Therefore the Son of man is Lord also of the sabbath.

In the Morning

O God, our Father, we give Thee thanks that today Thou art calling us to worship Thee and to learn of Thee.

Thou knowest the needs with which we will go to Thy house.

Grant that in it we may find comfort for sorrow, and soothing for the hearts that are sore.

Grant that in it we may find guidance for problems, and light for minds which are perplexed.

Grant that in it we may find strength for our temptations, and grace to overcome the fascination of the wrong things.

Grant that in it we may meet Jesus, and to go out not to forget Him any more.

Remember those who cannot go to Church today; those who are ill; those who are aged; those who are too sad to come; those who have the care of children and of family things; those who are nursing invalids; those who must work even today; those who will listen to the wireless services. And grant that in their own homes, in the hospitals, the infirmaries, the nursing-homes, as they journey, all such may know the unseen fellowship of the worshipping company of those who love Thee: through Jesus Christ our Lord.   AMEN.

In the Evening

O God, our Father, we thank Thee for all that Thou hast said to us and done for us today.

Grant that Thy word may not return unto Thee void
and empty, but that it may accomplish that for which
Thou didst send it.

Grant that tomorrow we may go back to our work with
bodies which are rested, minds which are enlightened,
and hearts which are more fully devoted to Thy love.

Grant that we may go back to the ordinary activities of
the world to see all life in the light of eternity, and to
judge all things by Thy presence.

O God, our Father, tonight we remember very specially
our absent friends. Wherever they are bless them,
and keep them safe.

Grant that tomorrow our walk may be closer to Thee,
and that there may be a clearer light to shine upon
the road which leads us to our journey's end: through
Jesus Christ our Lord.   AMEN.

Daily Reading

PSALM 118: 19–24

OPEN TO me the gates of righteousness: I will go into
them, and I will praise the Lord:

This gate of the Lord, into which the righteous shall
enter.

I will praise thee: for thou hast heard me, and art
become my salvation.

The stone which the builders refused is become the head
stone of the corner.

This is the Lord's doing; it is marvellous in our eyes.

This is the day which the Lord hath made; we will
rejoice and be glad in it.

PRAYERS WITH BIBLE READINGS
FOR FESTIVAL DAYS

THE FIRST DAY OF THE YEAR

In the Morning

Eternal and everblessed God, who makest all things new, we thank Thee that today Thou hast allowed us to begin a new year.

Here in Thy presence we make our resolutions for the days to come.

We resolve to be faithful and true to those who love us, and loyal to those who are our friends, so that we may never bring worry to their minds or distress to their hearts.

We resolve to live in forgiveness and in kindness, that, like our Master, we may go about ever doing good.

We resolve to live in diligence and in effort, that we may use to the full the gifts and the talents which Thou hast given unto us.

We resolve to live in goodness and in purity, that we ourselves may resist temptation, and that we may be a strength to others who are tempted.

We resolve to live in sympathy and in gentleness, that we may bring comfort to the sorrowing and understanding to the perplexed.

We resolve to live in serenity and in self-control, that no anger and no passion may disturb our own peace and the peace of others.

We resolve to live in full obedience and in perfect love to Thee, that in doing Thy will we may find our peace.

O God, our Father, who hast given us grace to make our resolutions, grant us also strength to keep them all this year: through Jesus Christ our Lord.

AMEN.

In the Evening

O God, our Father, already we have come to the end of the first day of this new year.

Help us never to forget how quickly time passes on its way, and so help us to use every moment of it to the utmost.

Help us to remember that opportunities come, and that often they never return, and so help us to seize them when they come.

Help us to remember that we never know when time will end for us, and so make us at all times to have all things ready to depart and to go to Thee.

O God, our Father, even this one day has shown us how hard it is to keep the resolutions which we have made. Help us to remember that without Thee we can do nothing, and so help us to walk each step with Thee, that in Thy protecting presence life may be safe from sin. This we ask for Thy love's sake.   AMEN.

Daily Reading

MATTHEW 28: 16–20

THEN THE eleven disciples went away into Galilee, into a mountain where Jesus had appointed them. And when they saw him, they worshipped him: but some doubted. And Jesus came and spake unto them, saying, All power is given unto me in heaven and in earth. Go ye therefore, and teach all nations, baptizing them in the name of the Father, and of the Son, and of the Holy Ghost: teaching them to observe all things whatsoever I have commanded you: and, lo, I am with you alway, even unto the end of the world. AMEN.

In the Morning

O God, our Father, we thank Thee this day that Thou didst so love the world that Thou didst give Thine only Son for us and for all mankind.

We give Thee thanks this day for Jesus Christ, our blessed Lord, and for His death upon the Cross.

That He was obedient unto death, even the death of the Cross;

That He loved us and gave Himself for us;

That He came to seek and to save that which was lost;

That He gave His life a ransom for many, a ransom for us:

We give Thee thanks this day, O God.

Greater love hath no man than this, that a man lay down his life for his friends. Help us this day to remember, and never again to forget, the love of Him who laid down His life for us.

> *O wondrous love! to bleed and die,*
> *To bear the Cross and shame,*
> *That guilty sinners, such as I,*
> *Might plead Thy gracious Name!*

Hear this our prayer, for Thy love's sake.   AMEN.

In the Evening

O Lord Jesus Christ, who didst say, I, if I be lifted up from the earth will draw all men unto me, fix our eyes this night upon Thy Cross.

Help us in Thy Cross to see the lengths to which man's sin will go. Help us in the Cross to see that sin is enmity to Thee, that sin is the destroyer of all beauty, and the enemy of all loveliness.

Help us in the Cross to see the lengths to which Thy love will go, that Thou didst love us so much that Thou didst keep nothing back.

Help us in the Cross to see the horror of sin, and to depart for ever from it.

Help us in the Cross to see the wonder of love, and to surrender for ever to it.

This we ask for Thy love's sake.   AMEN.

Daily Reading

JOHN 19: 14–18

AND IT was the preparation of the passover, and about the sixth hour: and Pilate saith unto the Jews, Behold your King! But they cried out, Away with him, away with him, crucify him. Pilate saith unto them, Shall I crucify your King? The chief priests answered, We have no king but Caesar. Then delivered he him therefore unto them to be crucified. And they took Jesus, and led him away. And he bearing his cross went forth into a place called the place of a skull, which is called in the Hebrew Golgotha: where they crucified him, and two other with him, on either side one, and Jesus in the midst.

In the Morning

O Lord Jesus Christ, who upon this day didst conquer death and rise from the dead, and who art alive for evermore, help us never to forget Thy Risen Presence for ever with us.

Help us to remember,
> That Thou art with us in every time of perplexity to guide and to direct;
> That Thou art with us in every time of sorrow to comfort and to console;
> That Thou art with us in every time of temptation to strengthen and to inspire;
> That Thou art with us in every time of loneliness to cheer and to befriend;
> That Thou art with us even in death to bring us through the waters to the glory on the other side.

Make us to be certain that there is nothing in time or in eternity which can separate us from Thee, so that in Thy presence we may meet life with gallantry and death without fear.

This we ask for Thy love's sake.   AMEN.

In the Evening

O Lord Jesus Christ, forgive us for the times when we have forgotten Thy Risen Presence for ever with us.

Forgive us for times when we failed in some task, because we did not ask Thy help.
Forgive us for times when we fell to some temptation, because we tried to meet it by ourselves.

Forgive us for times when we were afraid, because we thought that we were alone in the dark.

Forgive us for times when we were driven to despair, because we were trying to fight the battle in our own unaided strength.

Forgive us for times when we said and did things which now we are ashamed to remember that Thou didst hear and Thou didst see.

Forgive us for times when death seemed very terrible, and the loss of loved ones beyond all bearing, because we forgot that Thou hadst conquered death.

Make us this night again to hear Thee say: Lo, I am with you alway even unto the end of the world, and in that promise grant unto us to find courage and strength to meet all things undismayed.

This we ask for Thy love's sake.   AMEN.

Daily Reading

LUKE 24: 1–6

Now UPON the first day of the week, very early in the morning, they came unto the sepulchre, bringing the spices which they had prepared, and certain others with them. And they found the stone rolled away from the sepulchre. And they entered in, and found not the body of the Lord Jesus. And it came to pass, as they were much perplexed thereabout, behold, two men stood by them in shining garments: and as they were afraid, and bowed down their faces to the earth, they said unto them, Why seek ye the living among the dead? He is not here, but is risen.

In the Morning

Eternal and everblessed God, who upon this day didst send Thy Spirit with power upon Thy people, let Thy Spirit be upon us.

Let Thy Spirit be in our minds, to guide our thoughts towards the truth.

Let Thy Spirit be in our hearts, to cleanse them from every evil and unclean desire.

Let Thy Spirit be upon our lips, to preserve us from all wrong speaking, and to help us by our words to commend Thee unto others.

Let Thy Spirit be upon our eyes, that they may find no delight in looking on forbidden things, but that they may be fixed on Jesus.

Let Thy Spirit be upon our hands that they may be faithful in work and eager in service.

Let Thy Spirit be upon our whole lives, that they may be strong with Thy power, wise with Thy wisdom, and beautiful with Thy love: through Jesus Christ our Lord.   AMEN.

In the Evening

Eternal and everblessed God, who dost send thy Spirit to be our teacher and our guide, help us never to be afraid to follow where Thy Spirit leads.

Help us never to be afraid of new truth, but always to open our minds to Thy Spirit's teaching.

Help us never to be afraid of courageous action, but ever to act without fear as Thy Spirit prompts.

Help us never to be afraid of the criticism or the persecution of men, but ever to be certain that it will be given unto us through Thy Spirit what we must do and what we must say to defend the faith.

Let Thy Spirit move within the hearts of all men, that He may inspire them to discover truth, to spread abroad beauty, and to live in love.

And grant unto us ourselves to yield ourselves wholly to Thy Spirit, that Thou mayest be able to equip us for Thy work, and to use us in Thy service: through Jesus Christ our Lord.   AMEN.

Daily Reading

JOHN 14: 15–17, 25–27

IF YE love me, keep my commandments. And I will pray the Father, and he shall give you another Comforter, that he may abide with you for ever; even the Spirit of truth; whom the world cannot receive, because it seeth him not, neither knoweth him: but ye know him; for he dwelleth with you, and shall be in you. These things have I spoken unto you, being yet present with you. But the Comforter, which is the Holy Ghost, whom the Father will send in my name, he shall teach you all things, and bring all things to your remembrance, whatsoever I have said unto you. Peace I leave with you, my peace I give unto you: not as the world giveth, give I unto you. Let not your heart be troubled, neither let it be afraid.

In the Morning

Eternal and everblessed God, we remember this day the unseen cloud of witnesses who compass us about. We remember the blessed dead who do rest from their labours, and whose works do follow them. And we give Thee thanks for all of them.

For parents who gave us life; who tended and cared for us in years when we were helpless to help ourselves; who toiled and sacrificed to give to us our chance in life; at whose knees we learned to pray, and from whose lips we first heard the name of Jesus:
> We give Thee thanks, O God.

For teachers who taught us;
For ministers of Thy gospel who instructed us in Thy truth and in Thy faith;
For all those who have been an example to us of what life should be;
For those whose influence on us will never cease, and whose names will never depart from our memory;
> We give Thee thanks, O God.

For the saints, the prophets and the martyrs;
For those who lived and died for the faith;
And, above all else, for Jesus, the captain of our salvation and the author and finisher of our faith:
> We give Thee thanks, O God.

Grant unto us in our day and generation to walk worthily of the heritage into which we have entered: through Jesus Christ our Lord. AMEN.

In the Evening

O God, our Father, we remember this day all those whom we have loved and lost awhile.

We remember those whom Thou didst take to Thyself full of years and honour.
We remember those whom in the midtime Thou didst call.
We remember those for whom the flower of life never had time to blossom.
We remember all those whose earthly course is ended, and who are in Thy nearer presence.

Take from us all sadness, and teach us to sorrow not as others who have no hope.
Turn our thoughts from the darkness of death to the life eternal; and grant unto us the sure certainty that one day we shall be reunited in Thy presence with those whom we have loved.

This we ask for Thy love's sake.   AMEN.

Daily Reading

HEBREWS 11: 39, 12: 2

AND THESE all, having obtained a good report through faith, received not the promise: God having provided some better thing for us, that they without us should not be made perfect. Wherefore seeing we also are compassed about with so great a cloud of witnesses, let us lay aside every weight, and the sin which doth so easily beset us, and let us run with patience the race that is set before us, looking unto Jesus the author and finisher of our faith; who for the joy that was set before him endured the cross, despising the shame, and is set down at the right hand of the throne of God.

In the Morning

O God, our Father, we thank Thee for Christmas time, and for all that it means to us.

We thank Thee that, when Jesus, Thy Son, came into this world, He came into a humble home.

We thank Thee that He had to grow up and to learn like any other boy.

We thank Thee that he did a good day's work, when He grew to manhood, as the carpenter in the village shop in Nazareth.

We thank Thee that He was tempted and tired, hungry and sad, just as we are.

We thank Thee that He was one with His brethren in all things, that He truly shared this life with its struggles and its toils, its sorrows and its joys, its trials and its temptations.

We thank Thee that He knew what it is to live in a home circle, just as we do ; to earn His living, just as we do ; to know friendship and to know the failure of friends, just as we know it.

We thank Thee for the service of His life ; the love of His death ; and the power of His Resurrection.

Grant, O God, that, when He comes to us, He may not find that there is no room in our hearts for Him ; but grant that this Christmas day He may enter into our hearts and abide there for evermore.

Hear this our prayer, for Thy love's sake.   AMEN.

In the Evening

O God, our Father, we thank Thee for the happiness of this Christmas Day.

For the presents we have received; for the happiness we have enjoyed; for the meals we have eaten together, the games we have played together, the talk we have had together,
We thank Thee, O God.

We thank Thee for the peace and goodwill which have been amongst us all today. Grant that they may not be something which lasts only for today; but grant that we may take the Christmas joy and the Christmas fellowship with us into all the ordinary days of life.

Now at evening time we specially remember those for whom Christmas has not been a happy time. Bless those to whom sorrow came, and for whom it was all the sorer, because it came at the time when everyone else was so happy. Bless those who have no friends, no homes, no family circle, no one to remember them; and be with them in their loneliness to comfort and to cheer them. O God, we thank Thee for today; help us to try to deserve all our happiness a little more. Through Jesus Christ our Lord.   AMEN.

Daily Reading

LUKE 2: 11–14

FOR UNTO you is born this day in the city of David a Saviour, which is Christ the Lord. And this shall be a sign unto you; Ye shall find the babe wrapped in swaddling clothes, lying in a manger. And suddenly there was with the angel a multitude of the heavenly host praising God, and saying, Glory to God in the highest, and on earth peace, good will toward men.

In the Morning

O God, our Father, today we are remembering all the way by which Thou hast brought us to this present hour, and we thank Thee for every step of it.

We thank Thee for every experience which has come to us, because we know that in it and through it all Thou hast been loving us with an everlasting love.

For gladness and for grief; for sorrow and for joy; for laughter and for tears; for silence and for song:
> We give Thee thanks, O God.

That Thou hast kept us in our going out and our coming in;
That Thou hast enabled us to do our work, and to earn our living;
That Thou hast brought us in safety to this present hour:
> We give Thee thanks, O God.

For any new things that we have learned, and for any new experiences through which we have passed;
If we can do our work a little better, and if we know life a little better;
For friends who are still closer to us, and for loved ones who are still more dear:
> We give Thee thanks, O God.

And today, as we remember the passing years, we thank Thee most of all for Jesus Christ, the same yesterday, today and for ever. Help us to go on, certain that, as Thou hast blessed the past, so the future is also for ever in Thy hands: through Jesus Christ our Lord.
> AMEN.

THE LAST DAY OF THE YEAR

In the Evening

O God, our Father, tonight we are looking back across the year which is passing from us now.

There is so much for which we need forgiveness.

For the time we have wasted; for the opportunities we have neglected; for the strength we have given to the wrong things; for all the mistakes we have made:
Forgive us, O God.

There is so much for which we ought to give Thee thanks.
For health and for strength; for protection in the time of danger; for healing in the time of illness; for upholding in the day of sorrow; for daily light and daily leading:
We thank Thee, O God.

Bless those for whom this has been a happy year, and make them to give the thanks to Thee. Bless those for whom this has been a sad year, and help them still to face the future with steady eyes. And help us in the year to come so to live that at the end of it we shall not only be one year older, but that we shall also be one year nearer Thee. This we ask for Thy love's sake. AMEN.

Daily Reading

PSALM 90: 12 and 17

So TEACH us to number our days, that we may apply our hearts unto wisdom.
And let the beauty of the Lord our God be upon us: and establish thou the work of our hands upon us; yea, the work of our hands establish thou it.

PRAYERS
FOR SPECIAL OCCASIONS
IN THE HOME

When a Child is Born

O God, our Father, we give Thee thanks for this little child who has come to us from Thee. Bless him now and through all the days of his life.

Protect him in the days of his helplessness; bring him in safety through childhood's dangers; and grant that he may grow to manhood, and do a good day's work, and witness for Thee.

Help us his parents so to love him and so to train him that we shall not fail in the trust which Thou hast given unto us, and that, even as Thou hast given him unto us, we may give him back in dedication unto Thee: through Jesus Christ our Lord.   AMEN.

When a Child goes to School

O God, our Father, our son is going to school for the first time today; and we cannot help being anxious at this first step away from home.

Keep him safe from all that would hurt him in body or harm him in mind.

Help him to be happy at school, and to know the joy of learning and playing together with other boys and girls.

Help him to learn well that he may grow up to stand on his own feet, to earn his own living, and to serve Thee and his fellow-men: through Jesus Christ our Lord.
AMEN.

When there is a Marriage in the Family

O God, our Father, whose greatest gift is love, bless ... and ... who today within Thy presence will take each other in marriage. We thank Thee that they have found such love and faith and trust in each other that they wish to take each other to have and to hold all the days of their life. Let nothing ever come between them, but throughout all the chances and the changes of life keep them for ever loving and for ever true. Keep them safe from illness, from poverty, from all trouble which would hurt them in any way. But, if any trial does come to them, grant that it may only drive them closer together and closer to Thee. Grant unto them through all their days the perfect love which many waters cannot quench and which is stronger than even death itself: through Jesus Christ our Lord.   AMEN.

In the Time of Illness

O God, our Father, bless and help . . . in the illness which has come upon him.

Give him courage and patience, endurance and cheerfulness to bear all weakness and all pain; and give him the mind at rest, which will make his recovery all the quicker.

Give to all doctors, surgeons and nurses who attend him skill on their hands, wisdom in their minds, and gentleness and sympathy in their hearts.

Help us not to worry too much, but to leave our loved one in the hands of wise and skilful men who have the gift of healing, and in Thy hands.

Lord Jesus, come to us and to our loved one this day and at this time, and show us that Thy healing touch has never lost its ancient power. This we ask for Thy love's sake.   AMEN.

In the Time of Sorrow

O God, our Father, we know that Thou art afflicted in all our afflictions; and in our sorrow we come to

Thee today that Thou mayest give to us the comfort which Thou alone canst give.

Make us to be sure that in perfect wisdom, perfect love, and perfect power Thou art working ever for the best.

Make us sure that a Father's hand will never cause His child a needless tear.

Make us so sure of Thy love that we will be able to accept even that which we cannot understand.

Help us today to be thinking not of the darkness of death, but of the splendour of the life everlasting, for ever in Thy presence and for ever with Thee.

Help us still to face life with grace and gallantry; and help us to find courage to go on in the memory that the best tribute we can pay to our loved one is not the tribute of tears, but the constant memory that another has been added to the unseen cloud of witnesses who compass us about.

Comfort and uphold us, strengthen and support us, until we also come to the green pastures which are beside the still waters, and until we meet again those whom we have loved and lost awhile: through Jesus Christ our Lord.   AMEN.

When Bad News comes

O God, our Father, whatever comes to us make us able to stand on our feet, and to face it with steady eyes. Help us to be sure that we will never be tried above that which we are able to bear. Help us to be sure that Thy grace is sufficient to make even our weakness able to face and to conquer anything that can come to us. Make us sure that in the valley of the deep dark shadow Thou art there to comfort and to support; and that when we pass through the waters Thou art there to hold us up, and to bring us through them to the other side: through Jesus Christ our Lord.   AMEN.

When Good News comes

O God, my Father, who hast portioned out all my life
for me, I thank Thee for the good news which has
come to me today. I thank Thee that Thou hast
given me success; that my hope is realised, that my
dream has come true, and that my ambition is
fulfilled. Keep me today and in the days to come
from all pride and from all self-conceit. Help me to
remember that without Thee I can do nothing. So
keep me all my days in humility and in gratitude to
Thee: through Jesus Christ our Lord.   AMEN.

In the Hour of Temptation

Lord Jesus, Thou knowest what temptation is like. Thou
knowest how strongly the wrong thing fascinates me,
and how much the forbidden thing attracts me. Lord
Jesus, help me not to fall.

Help me to remember my own self-respect, and to remember that I cannot do a thing like this.

Help me to think of those who love me, and to know
that I dare not bring disappointment and heartbreak
to them.

Help me to remember the unseen cloud of witnesses who
compass me about, and to know that I cannot grieve
those who have passed on, but who are for ever near.

Help me to remember Thy presence, and in Thy presence
to find my safety. This I ask for Thy love's sake.

AMEN.

In the Time of Decision

O God, Thou knowest that today I must make a decision
which is going to affect my whole life. Help me to
choose the right way. Grant me Thy guidance, and
with it grant me the humble obedience to accept it.
Help me not to choose what I want to do, but what

Thou dost wish me to do. Grant that I may not be swayed by fear or by hope of gain, by selfish love of ease or comfort or by personal ambition, by the desire to escape or the longing for prestige. Help me today in humble obedience to say to Thee : " Lord, what wilt Thou have me to do ? " and then to await Thy guidance, and to accept Thy leading. Hear this my prayer, and send me an answer so clear that I cannot mistake it. This I ask for Thy love's sake.

AMEN.

In the Time of Journeying and Separation

O God, our Father, beyond whose love and care we cannot drift, bless . . . in his journeying today. Bring him in safety to his journey's end ; and let no ill befall him in body, mind or spirit. Grant that, when we are separated from each other, we may ever remember that, though we are absent from one another, we are still present with Thee. And keep us true and faithful to each other until we meet again : through Jesus Christ our Lord. AMEN.

Before going on Holiday

O God, our Father, we thank Thee for this time of rest from our daily work and our daily business.
We thank Thee for time to spend with our family and in the circle of those most dear.
We thank Thee for the open road, and the hills and the sea-shore, and for the clean wind upon our faces.
We thank Thee for games to play, for new places to see, new people to meet, new things to do.
Grant that the days of our holiday may refresh us in body and in mind, so that we may come back to work the better, because we rested awhile : through Jesus Christ our Lord. AMEN.

In the Time of Disappointment

O God, my Father, Thou knowest the disappointment which has come to me today; and Thou knowest that that which I wished for and longed for has not come to me. Keep me from feeling resentful and bitter. Keep me from feeling ill-used and from developing a grudge against life.

Keep me from being jealous and envious of those who have entered into that which was denied to me. Keep me from wasting my time in vain regrets, and from making myself wretched and making others unhappy.

Help me to count the blessings that I have. Help me to serve Thee and to serve my fellow-men with my whole heart in whatsoever place life has set me, and in whatsoever work has been given me to do: through Jesus Christ our Lord. AMEN.

After a Quarrel

O God, Thou knowest that today I have broken Thy commandment of love, and that I have parted with my brother man in anger. Even if I have been wronged and insulted, teach me how to forgive. Even if I was right, help me to make the first approach and to take the first step to putting things right again. Keep me from foolish pride and from nursing my foolish anger. Help me to be looking at Jesus, that in Him I may see the example of how to forgive, and that in Him I may find the will and the power to forgive: this I ask for Thy love's sake. AMEN.

In a Time of Worry and Anxiety

O God, Thou knowest how worried and anxious I am about . . .

Help me to be sensible, and to see that worrying about things does not make them any better.

Help me to be trustful, and to do all that I can, and then to leave the rest to Thee.

Help me to be sure that nothing can happen to me through which Thou canst not bring me in safety; and that nothing can separate me from Thy love.

Help me to lose my anxiety in the certainty that the everlasting arms are underneath me and about me; and give me something of the peace which the world cannot give, and cannot ever take away: through Jesus Christ our Lord.   AMEN.

When we come to the End
of our Working Days

O God, today I am going out to my work for the last time. I thank Thee for all the years of work which Thou hast enabled me to do. I thank Thee for the strenuous working years of my life, and now I thank Thee that Thou hast given to me a time for rest. Help me to lay down my work gratefully and graciously and not grudgingly and resentfully, and not to be envious and jealous of the younger people who are stepping into my place. In the days to come keep me from rusting in idleness. Keep me still interested in life; still of service to others; still finding something to do; still learning; and still happy to the very end: through Jesus Christ our Lord.   AMEN.

When we have made mistakes and
fallen to temptation

O God, my Father, Thou knowest that today I have fallen to temptation and that I have done wrong. I have brought shame to myself, anxiety to those who love me, and grief to Thee. O God, in Thy mercy, forgive me for Jesus' sake. Help me to be brave enough not only to confess this sin to Thee and to ask Thy forgiveness, but to ask the forgiveness of the person

I have hurt and wronged and injured, and to do all I can to put things right again. Keep me from too much regret, too much remorse, and help me to rise above the error I have made and the wrong that I have done. In the days to come help me not to make the same mistake again. Give me a conscience which is quick and tender, and give me grace always to obey it. Help me to walk with Jesus that in His company I may be saved from sin and enabled to do the right. This I ask for Thy love's sake.   AMEN.

BIBLE READINGS
THROUGHOUT THE YEAR

Notes

1. These readings are alternative to those printed in full with the prayers for each day and provide anyone making regular use of *The Plain Man's Book of Prayers*, month by month, with fresh reading material covering a full year.

2. Each day one of the two readings is from the Gospels. If only morning or only evening readings are followed two Gospels will be read through in the course of one year. If both readings are used each day, all four Gospels will be read through in the course of one year.

3. Readings vary a good deal in length. The endeavour has been to make each one something of a unity in itself.

	MORNING		EVENING

FIRST DAY

	MORNING		EVENING
January	Mt. 3: 1–6	*January*	Gen. 1: 1–5
February	Ex. 1: 1–14	*February*	Lk. 3: 1–9
March	Mt. 10: 1–15	*March*	Rom. 1: 1–12
April	I Cor. 1: 10–18	*April*	Lk. 10: 1–16
May	Mt. 18: 1–6	*May*	Jud. 7: 13–23
June	I Kings 2: 1–4	*June*	Lk. 18: 1–8
July	Mt. 26: 1–16	*July*	Acts 1: 1–9
August	Acts 13: 1–12	*August*	Jn. 1: 1–14
September	Mk. 5: 1–13	*September*	Eph. 1: 1–12
October	Heb. 1: 1–12	*October*	Jn. 8: 1–11
November	Mk. 11: 1–11	*November*	Jer. 1: 1–10
December	Is. 2: 1–5	*December*	Jn. 17: 1–10

SECOND DAY

	MORNING		EVENING
January	Mt. 3: 7–12	*January*	Gen. 1: 26–31
February	Ex. 1: 15–22	*February*	Lk. 3: 10–22
March	Mt. 10: 16–25	*March*	Rom. 1: 13–17
April	I Cor. 1: 22–31	*April*	Lk. 10: 17–24
May	Mt. 18: 7–14	*May*	Jud. 16: 4–14
June	I Kings 3: 5–15	*June*	Lk. 18: 9–17
July	Mt. 26: 17–30	*July*	Acts 1: 10–14

MORNING   EVENING

SECOND DAY *continued*

August	Acts 13: 26–31	*August*	Jn. 1: 15–28
September	Mk. 5: 14–20	*September*	Eph. 1: 15–23
October	Heb. 2: 1–4	*October*	Jn. 8: 12–20
November	Mk. 11: 12–19	*November*	Jer. 2: 9–13
December	Is. 5: 1–7	*December*	Jn. 17: 11–19

THIRD DAY

January	Mt. 3: 13–17	*January*	Gen. 12: 1–8
February	Ex. 2: 1–10	*February*	Lk. 4: 1–13
March	Mt. 10: 26–33	*March*	Rom. 5: 1–8
April	I Cor. 3: 1–9	*April*	Lk. 10: 25–37
May	Mt. 18: 15–20	*May*	Jud. 16: 15–22
June	I Kings 6: 1–14	*June*	Lk. 18: 18–30
July	Mt. 26: 31–46	*July*	Acts 1: 15–26
August	Acts 13: 44–52	*August*	Jn. 1: 29–34
September	Mk. 5: 21–34	*September*	Eph. 2: 1–7
October	Heb. 3: 1–6	*October*	Jn. 8: 21–32
November	Mk. 11: 20–26	*November*	Jer. 18: 1–11
December	Is. 6: 1–8	*December*	Jn. 17: 20–26

FOURTH DAY

January	Mt. 4: 1–11	*January*	Gen. 17: 1–8
February	Ex. 2: 11–25	*February*	Lk. 4: 14–30
March	Mt. 10: 34–42	*March*	Rom. 5: 9–21
April	I Cor. 3: 16–23	*April*	Lk. 10: 38–42
May	Mt. 18: 21–35	*May*	Jud. 16: 23–30
June	I Kings 8: 22–30	*June*	Lk. 18: 31–43
July	Mt. 26: 47–56	*July*	Acts 2: 1–11
August	Acts 14: 8–18	*August*	Jn. 1: 35–42
September	Mk. 5: 35–43	*September*	Eph. 2: 8–13
October	Heb. 4: 12–16	*October*	Jn. 8: 33–46
November	Mk. 11: 27–33	*November*	Jer. 23: 1–8
December	Is. 9: 1–7	*December*	Jn. 18: 1–14

FIFTH DAY

January	Mt. 4: 12–17	*January*	Gen. 18: 20–33
February	Ex. 3: 1–10	*February*	Lk. 4: 31–37
March	Mt. 11: 1–6	*March*	Rom. 6: 1–11
April	I Cor. 9: 16–27	*April*	Lk. 11: 1–13
May	Mt. 19: 1–9	*May*	Ruth 1: 1–10
June	I Kings 9: 1–9	*June*	Lk. 19: 1–10
July	Mt. 26: 57–68	*July*	Acts 2: 12–21

MORNING	EVENING

FIFTH DAY *continued*

August	Acts 14: 19–28	*August*	Jn. 1: 43–51
September	Mk. 6: 1–6	*September*	Eph. 2: 14–22
October	Heb. 10: 19–25	*October*	Jn. 8: 47–59
November	Mk. 12: 1–12	*November*	Jer. 31: 31–34
December	Is. 11: 1–9	*December*	Jn. 18: 15–27

SIXTH DAY

January	Mt. 4: 18–25	*January*	Gen. 22: 1–18
February	Ex. 3: 11–17	*February*	Lk. 4: 38–44
March	Mt. 11: 7–19	*March*	Rom. 6: 16–23
April	I Cor. 10: 12–17	*April*	Lk. 11: 14–26
May	Mt. 19: 10–15	*May*	Ruth 1: 16–22
June	I Kings 17: 1–6	*June*	Lk. 19: 11–27
July	Mt. 26: 69–75	*July*	Acts 2: 22–36
August	Acts 16: 6–12	*August*	Jn. 2: 1–11
September	Mk. 6: 7–13	*September*	Eph. 3: 14–21
October	Heb. 11: 1–10	*October*	Jn. 9: 1–7
November	Mk. 12: 13–17	*November*	Ezl. 3: 4–14
December	Is. 12: 1–6	*December*	Jn. 18: 28–40

SEVENTH DAY

January	Mt. 5: 1–12	*January*	Gen. 28: 10–22
February	Ex. 5: 1–9	*February*	Lk. 5: 1–11
March	Mt. 11: 20–30	*March*	Rom. 7: 14–25
April	I Cor. 11: 23–36	*April*	Lk. 11: 27–36
May	Mt. 19: 16–22	*May*	Ruth 2: 1–12
June	I Kings 17: 8–16	*June*	Lk. 19: 28–40
July	Mt. 27: 1–14	*July*	Acts 2: 37–47
August	Acts 16: 14–24	*August*	Jn. 2: 12–17
September	Mk. 6: 14–29	*September*	Eph. 4: 1–7
October	Heb. 11: 32–40	*October*	Jn. 9: 8–23
November	Mk. 12: 18–27	*November*	Ezl. 34: 11–15
December	Is. 25: 1–9	*December*	Jn. 19: 1–12

EIGHTH DAY

January	Mt. 5: 13–16	*January*	Gen. 32: 24–32
February	Ex. 5: 10–23	*February*	Lk. 5: 12–15
March	Mt. 12: 1–8	*March*	Rom. 8: 1–6
April	I Cor. 12: 1–13	*April*	Lk. 11: 37–44
May	Mt. 19: 23–30	*May*	I Sam. 3: 1–10
June	I Kings 17: 17–24	*June*	Lk. 19: 41–48
July	Mt. 27: 15–26	*July*	Acts 3: 1–8

MORNING	EVENING

EIGHTH DAY *continued*

August	Acts 16: 25–40	*August*	Jn. 2: 18–25
September	Mk. 6: 30–34	*September*	Eph. 4: 11–16
October	Heb. 12: 1–6	*October*	Jn. 9: 24–41
November	Mk. 12: 28–34	*November*	Ezl. 34: 22–31
December	Is. 26: 1–4	*December*	Jn. 19: 13–18

NINTH DAY

January	Mt. 5: 17–20	*January*	Gen. 35: 1–7
February	Ex. 7: 1–13	*February*	Lk. 5: 16–26
March	Mt. 12: 9–21	*March*	Rom. 8: 14–18
April	I Cor. 12: 14–27	*April*	Lk. 11: 45–54
May	Mt. 20: 1–16	*May*	I Sam. 3: 11–19
June	I Kings 18: 17–21	*June*	Lk. 20: 1–8
July	Mt. 27: 27–38	*July*	Acts 3: 12–18
August	Acts 17: 1–15	*August*	Jn. 3: 1–13
September	Mk. 6: 35–44	*September*	Eph. 4: 17–25
October	Jam. 1: 1–12	*October*	Jn. 10: 1–16
November	Mk. 12: 35–40	*November*	Ezl. 36: 22–28
December	Is. 35: 1–10	*December*	Jn. 19: 19–24

TENTH DAY

January	Mt. 5: 21–26	*January*	Gen. 37: 1–11
February	Ex. 7: 14–25	*February*	Lk. 5: 27–32
March	Mt. 12: 22–30	*March*	Rom. 8: 22–28
April	I Cor. 13: 1–13	*April*	Lk. 12: 1–12
May	Mt. 20: 17–28	*May*	I Sam. 7: 3–12
June	I Kings 18: 22–39	*June*	Lk. 20: 9–18
July	Mt. 27: 39–56	*July*	Acts 3: 19–26
August	Acts 17: 16–21	*August*	Jn. 3: 14–21
September	Mk. 6: 45–56	*September*	Eph. 4: 26–32
October	Jam. 1: 13–27	*October*	Jn. 10: 17–30
November	Mk. 12: 41–44	*November*	Ezl. 37: 1–14
December	Is. 40: 1–8	*December*	Jn. 19: 25–30

ELEVENTH DAY

January	Mt. 5: 27–32	*January*	Gen. 37: 12–22
February	Ex. 11: 1–10	*February*	Lk. 5: 33–39
March	Mt. 12: 31–37	*March*	Rom. 8: 31–39
April	I Cor. 14: 1–12	*April*	Lk. 12: 13–21
May	Mt. 20: 29–34	*May*	I Sam. 7: 13–17
June	I Kings 19: 1–8	*June*	Lk. 20: 19–26
July	Mt. 27: 57–66	*July*	Acts 4: 1–12

MORNING   EVENING

ELEVENTH DAY *continued*

August	Acts 17: 22–34	*August*	Jn. 3: 22–36
September	Mk. 7: 1–13	*September*	Eph. 5: 6–13
October	Jam. 2: 14–26	*October*	Jn. 10: 31–42
November	Mk. 13: 1–10	*November*	Dan. 3: 8–18
December	Is. 40: 9–11	*December*	Jn. 19: 31–37

TWELFTH DAY

January	Mt. 5: 33–37	*January*	Gen. 37: 23–28
February	Ex. 12: 1–14	*February*	Lk. 6: 1–19
March	Mt. 12: 38–45	*March*	Rom. 9: 21–26
April	I Cor. 15: 1–11	*April*	Lk. 12: 22–31
May	Mt. 21: 1–11	*May*	I Sam. 9: 1–10
June	I Kings 19: 9–16	*June*	Lk. 20: 27–38
July	Mt. 28: 1–10	*July*	Acts 4: 13–22
August	Acts 18: 1–11	*August*	Jn. 4: 1–15
September	Mk. 7: 14–23	*September*	Eph. 5: 14–21
October	Jam. 3: 1–10	*October*	Jn. 11: 1–16
November	Mk. 13: 11–23	*November*	Dan. 3: 19–25
December	Is. 40: 25–31	*December*	Jn. 19: 38–42

THIRTEENTH DAY

January	Mt. 5: 38–42	*January*	Gen. 37: 29–36
February	Ex. 12: 29–36	*February*	Lk. 6: 20–38
March	Mt. 12: 46–50	*March*	Rom. 10: 1–11
April	I Cor. 15: 12–22	*April*	Lk. 12: 32–40
May	Mt. 21: 12–16	*May*	I Sam. 9: 11–17
June	II Kings 2: 9–15	*June*	Lk. 20: 39–47
July	Mt. 28: 11–15	*July*	Acts 4: 23–30
August	Acts 18: 24–28	*August*	Jn. 4: 16–26
September	Mk. 7: 24–30	*September*	Eph. 6: 10–20
October	Jam. 5: 10–16	*October*	Jn. 11: 17–32
November	Mk. 13: 24–31	*November*	Dan. 6: 4–10
December	Is. 41: 8–13	*December*	Jn. 20: 1–10

FOURTEENTH DAY

January	Mt. 5: 43–48	*January*	Gen. 39: 1–6
February	Ex. 14: 5–14	*February*	Lk. 6: 39–49
March	Mt. 13: 1–23	*March*	Rom. 10: 12–17
April	I Cor. 15: 35–50	*April*	Lk. 12: 41–48
May	Mt. 21: 17–22	*May*	I Sam. 10: 1–11
June	II Kings 4: 18–37	*June*	Lk. 21: 1–4
July	Mt. 28: 16–20	*July*	Acts 4: 31–37

MORNING   EVENING

FOURTEENTH DAY *continued*

	MORNING		EVENING
August	Acts 19: 1–10	*August*	Jn. 4: 27–38
September	Mk. 7: 31–37	*September*	Phil. 1: 1–11
October	I Pet. 1: 3–9	*October*	Jn. 11: 33–46
November	Mk. 13: 32–37	*November*	Dan. 6: 11–23
December	Is. 42: 1–9	*December*	Jn. 20: 11–18

FIFTEENTH DAY

	MORNING		EVENING
January	Mt. 6: 1–6	*January*	Gen. 41: 1–8
February	Ex. 14: 15–31	*February*	Lk. 7: 1–10
March	Mt. 13: 24–30	*March*	Rom. 11: 25–36
April	I Cor. 15: 51–58	*April*	Lk. 12: 49–59
May	Mt. 21: 23–32	*May*	I Sam. 10: 17–24
June	II Kings 5: 1–14	*June*	Lk. 21: 5–24
July	Mk. 1: 1–11	*July*	Acts 5: 17–26
August	Acts 19: 11–20	*August*	Jn. 4: 39–42
September	Mk. 8: 1–9	*September*	Phil. 1: 12–20
October	I Pet. 1: 13–25	*October*	Jn. 11: 47–57
November	Mk. 14: 1–9	*November*	Dan. 12: 1–4
December	Is. 43: 1–7	*December*	Jn. 20: 19–31

SIXTEENTH DAY

	MORNING		EVENING
January	Mt. 6: 7–15	*January*	Gen. 41: 9–13
February	Ex. 15: 1–19	*February*	Lk. 7: 11–17
March	Mt. 13: 31–43	*March*	Rom. 12: 1–9
April	I Cor. 16: 1–13	*April*	Lk. 13: 1–9
May	Mt. 21: 33–46	*May*	I Sam. 12: 1–15
June	II Kings 6: 8–23	*June*	Lk. 21: 25–38
July	Mk. 1: 12–20	*July*	Acts 5: 27–32
August	Acts 20: 6–12	*August*	Jn. 4: 43–54
September	Mk. 8: 10–21	*September*	Phil. 1: 21–30
October	I Pet. 2: 1–10	*October*	Jn. 12: 1–11
November	Mk. 14: 10–21	*November*	Hos. 14: 1–9
December	Is. 49: 7–13	*December*	Jn. 21: 1–14

SEVENTEENTH DAY

	MORNING		EVENING
January	Mt. 6: 16–24	*January*	Gen. 41: 14–36
February	Ex. 16: 1–15	*February*	Lk. 7: 18–30
March	Mt. 13: 44–52	*March*	Rom. 12: 10–21
April	II Cor. 1: 8–14	*April*	Lk. 13: 10–17
May	Mt. 22: 1–10	*May*	I Sam. 12: 16–25
June	II Kings 18: 1–8	*June*	Lk. 22: 1–20
July	Mk. 1: 21–28	*July*	Acts 5: 33–42

MORNING   EVENING

SEVENTEENTH DAY *continued*

August	Acts 20: 17–27	*August*	Jn. 5: 1–9
September	Mk. 8: 22–26	*September*	Phil. 2: 1–11
October	I Pet. 3: 8–13	*October*	Jn. 12: 12–19
November	Mk. 14: 22–25	*November*	Joel 2: 28–32
December	Is. 51: 9–16	*December*	Jn. 21: 15–25

EIGHTEENTH DAY

January	Mt. 6: 25–34	*January*	Gen. 41: 37–45
February	Ex. 17: 1–5	*February*	Lk. 7: 31–35
March	Mt. 13: 53–58	*March*	Rom. 13: 1–9
April	II Cor. 3: 1–6	*April*	Lk. 13: 18–30
May	Mt. 22: 11–22	*May*	I Sam. 16: 1–13
June	II Kings 22: 3–13	*June*	Lk. 22: 21–38
July	Mk. 1: 29–34	*July*	Acts 6: 1–8
August	Acts 20: 28–38	*August*	Jn. 5: 10–16
September	Mk. 8: 27–33	*September*	Phil. 2: 12–18
October	I Pet. 4: 12–16	*October*	Jn. 12: 20–36
November	Mk. 14: 26–31	*November*	Amos 3: 1–8
December	Is. 52: 1–6	*December*	Lk. 1: 1–17

NINETEENTH DAY

January	Mt. 7: 1–5	*January*	Gen. 41: 46–57
February	Ex. 17: 8–16	*February*	Lk. 7: 36–50
March	Mt. 14: 1–13	*March*	Rom. 13: 10–14
April	II Cor. 4: 1–7	*April*	Lk. 13: 31–35
May	Mt. 22: 23–33	*May*	I Sam. 16: 14–23
June	II Kings 23: 1–30	*June*	Lk. 22: 39–46
July	Mk. 1: 35–45	*July*	Acts 6: 9–15
August	Acts 21: 8–17	*August*	Jn. 5: 17–31
September	Mk. 8: 34–38	*September*	Phil. 3: 1–11
October	II Pet. 3: 8–18	*October*	Jn. 12: 37–43
November	Mk. 14: 32–42	*November*	Amos 5: 4–8
December	Is. 52: 7–10	*December*	Lk. 1: 18–25

TWENTIETH DAY

January	Mt. 7: 6–12	*January*	Gen. 42: 1–20
February	Ex. 19: 1–9	*February*	Lk. 8: 1–15
March	Mt. 14: 14–21	*March*	Rom. 14: 1–9
April	II Cor. 4: 8–18	*April*	Lk. 14: 1–11
May	Mt. 22: 34–40	*May*	I Sam. 17: 1–11
June	II Kings 23: 21–25	*June*	Lk. 22: 47–62
July	Mk. 2: 1–12	*July*	Acts 7: 51–60

MORNING	EVENING

TWENTIETH DAY *continued*

August	Acts 21: 27–36	*August*	Jn. 5: 32–47
September	Mk. 9: 1–10	*September*	Phil. 3: 12–21
October	I Jn. 1: 5–9	*October*	Jn. 12: 44–50
November	Mk. 14: 43–52	*November*	Amos 5: 14–24
December	Is. 53: 1–12	*December*	Lk. 1: 26–38

TWENTY-FIRST DAY

January	Mt. 7: 13–20	*January*	Gen. 42: 21–38
February	Ex. 20: 1–17	*February*	Lk. 8: 16–21
March	Mt. 14: 22–36	*March*	Rom. 14: 10–18
April	II Cor. 5: 14–21	*April*	Lk. 14: 12–24
May	Mt. 22: 41–46	*May*	I Sam. 17: 32–37
June	II Kings 24: 10–16	*June*	Lk. 22: 63–71
July	Mk. 2: 13–17	*July*	Acts 8: 1–8
August	Acts 22: 1–16	*August*	Jn. 6: 1–14
September	Mk. 9: 11–29	*September*	Phil. 4: 1–7
October	I Jn. 2: 1–5	*October*	Jn. 13: 1–17
November	Mk. 14: 53–65	*November*	Amos 8: 4–12
December	Is. 55: 1–5	*December*	Lk. 1: 39–45

TWENTY-SECOND DAY

January	Mt. 7: 21–29	*January*	Gen. 43: 1–14
February	Deut. 6: 1–9	*February*	Lk. 8: 22–25
March	Mt. 15: 1–11	*March*	Rom. 15: 1–7
April	II Cor. 9: 1–7	*April*	Lk. 14: 25–35
May	Mt. 23: 1–12	*May*	I Sam. 17: 38–51
June	Ezra 1: 1–11	*June*	Lk. 23: 1–12
July	Mk. 2: 18–22	*July*	Acts 8: 26–40
August	Acts 25: 1–12	*August*	Jn. 6: 15–21
September	Mk. 9: 30–37	*September*	Phil. 4: 8–13
October	I Jn. 3: 1–11	*October*	Jn. 13: 18–30
November	Mk. 14: 66–72	*November*	Amos 9: 11–15
December	Is. 55: 6–13	*December*	Lk. 1: 46–55

TWENTY-THIRD DAY

January	Mt. 8: 1–13	*January*	Gen. 43: 15–25
February	Deut. 6: 20–25	*February*	Lk. 8: 26–39
March	Mt. 15: 12–20	*March*	Rom. 15: 8–13
April	II Cor. 9: 8–15	*April*	Lk. 15: 1–10
May	Mt. 23: 13–24	*May*	I Sam. 18: 1–9
June	Ezra 3: 8–13	*June*	Lk. 23: 13–26
July	Mk. 2: 23–27	*July*	Acts 9: 1–9

MORNING	EVENING

TWENTY-THIRD DAY *continued*

August	Acts 25: 13–22	*August*	Jn. 6: 22–35
September	Mk. 9: 38–50	*September*	Col. 1: 1–8
October	I Jn. 4: 7–15	*October*	Jn. 13: 31–38
November	Mk. 15: 1–15	*November*	Mic. 4: 1–5
December	Is. 60: 1–9	*December*	Lk. 1: 56–66

TWENTY-FOURTH DAY

January	Mt. 8: 14–22	*January*	Gen. 43: 26–34
February	Deut. 30: 15–20	*February*	Lk. 8: 40–56
March	Mt. 15: 21–28	*March*	I Thes. 1: 1–10
April	II Cor. 10: 7–18	*April*	Lk. 15: 11–32
May	Mt. 23: 25–39	*May*	I Sam. 19: 1–12
June	Ezra 6: 15–22	*June*	Lk. 23: 27–38
July	Mk. 3: 1–12	*July*	Acts 9: 10–18
August	Acts 25: 23–27	*August*	Jn. 6: 36–47
September	Mk. 10: 1–12	*September*	Col. 1: 9–17
October	I Jn. 4: 16–21	*October*	Jn. 14: 1–14
November	Mk. 15: 16–21	*November*	Mic. 5: 1–4
December	Is. 60: 18–22	*December*	Lk. 1: 67–80

TWENTY-FIFTH DAY

January	Mt. 8: 23–27	*January*	Gen. 44: 1–13
February	Deut. 31: 1–8	*February*	Lk. 9: 1–17
March	Mt. 15: 29–39	*March*	I Thes. 1: 13–20
April	II Cor. 12: 1–9	*April*	Lk. 16: 1–12
May	Mt. 24: 1–13	*May*	I Sam. 26: 1–12
June	Neh. 1: 1–11	*June*	Lk. 23: 39–49
July	Mk. 3: 13–20	*July*	Acts 9: 23–31
August	Acts 26: 1–15	*August*	Jn. 6: 48–58
September	Mk. 10: 13–16	*September*	Col. 1: 18–29
October	I Jn. 5: 1–6	*October*	Jn. 14: 15–24
November	Mk. 15: 22–32	*November*	Mic. 6: 1–8
December	Mt. 1: 18–25	*December*	Lk. 2: 1–14

TWENTY-SIXTH DAY

January	Mt. 8: 28–34	*January*	Gen. 44: 14–34
February	Josh. 1: 1–9	*February*	Lk. 9: 18–27
March	Mt. 16: 1–12	*March*	I Thes. 4: 13–18
April	Gal. 3: 1–14	*April*	Lk. 16: 13–18
May	Mt. 24: 14–35	*May*	II Sam. 1: 17–27
June	Neh. 2: 1–11	*June*	Lk. 23: 50–56
July	Mk. 3: 21–30	*July*	Acts 9: 36–43

MORNING **EVENING**

TWENTY-SIXTH DAY *continued*

August	Acts 26: 19–32	*August*	Jn. 6: 59–71
September	Mk. 10: 17–22	*September*	Col. 2: 1–7
October	Rev. 1: 4–8	*October*	Jn. 14: 25–31
November	Mk. 15: 33–39	*November*	Zeph. 3: 14–20
December	Mt. 2: 1–10	*December*	Lk. 2: 15–20

TWENTY-SEVENTH DAY

January	Mt. 9: 1–8	*January*	Gen. 45: 1–15
February	Josh. 3: 9–17	*February*	Lk. 9: 28–36
March	Mt. 16: 13–20	*March*	I Thes. 5: 1–11
April	Gal. 3: 24–29	*April*	Lk. 16: 19–31
May	Mt. 24: 36–44	*May*	II Sam. 5: 1–10
June	Neh. 2: 12–20	*June*	Lk. 24: 1–12
July	Mk. 3: 31–35	*July*	Acts 10: 1–18
August	Acts 27: 1–11	*August*	Jn. 7: 1–13
September	Mk. 10: 23–27	*September*	Col. 2: 8–12
October	Rev. 3: 14–22	*October*	Jn. 15: 1–13
November	Mk. 15: 40–47	*November*	Zach. 9: 9–14
December	Mt. 2: 11–15	*December*	Lk. 2: 21–32

TWENTY-EIGHTH DAY

January	Mt. 9: 9–13	*January*	Gen. 45: 16–28
February	Josh. 24: 1–15	*February*	Lk. 9: 37–50
March	Mt. 16: 21–28	*March*	I Thes. 5: 12–28
April	Gal. 5: 16–26	*April*	Lk. 17: 1–10
May	Mt. 24: 45–51	*May*	II Sam. 9: 1–13
June	Neh. 4: 1–6	*June*	Lk. 24: 13–27
July	Mk. 4: 1–20	*July*	Acts 10: 19–33
August	Acts 27: 14–26	*August*	Jn. 7: 14–24
September	Mk. 10: 28–34	*September*	Col. 3: 1–11
October	Rev. 7: 9–17	*October*	Jn. 15: 14–27
November	Mk. 16: 1–8	*November*	Mal. 3: 1–6
December	Mt. 2: 16–23	*December*	Lk. 2: 33–40

TWENTY-NINTH DAY

January	Mt. 9: 14–17	*January*	Gen. 46: 1–7
February	Josh. 24: 16–25	*February*	Lk. 9: 51–62
March	Mt. 17: 1–13	*March*	II Thes. 3: 1–5
April	Gal. 6: 1–9	*April*	Lk. 17: 11–19
May	Mt. 25: 1–13	*May*	II Sam. 18: 24–33
June	Neh. 4: 7–18	*June*	Lk. 24: 28–35
July	Mk. 4: 21–29	*July*	Acts 10: 34–48

MORNING	EVENING

TWENTY-NINTH DAY *continued*

	MORNING			EVENING
August	Acts 27: 27–44		*August*	Jn. 7: 25–31
September	Mk. 10: 35–45		*September*	Col. 3: 12–17
October	Rev. 21: 1–7		*October*	Jn. 16: 1–14
November	Mk. 16: 9–14		*November*	Mal. 3: 7–10
December	Is. 61: 1–6		*December*.	Lk. 2: 41–52

THIRTIETH DAY

	MORNING			EVENING
January	Mt. 9: 18–38		*January*	Gen. 47: 1–12
February			*February*	
March	Mt. 17: 14–27		*March*	I Tim. 6: 12–19
April	Gal. 6: 10–18		*April*	Lk. 17: 20–37
May	Mt. 25: 14–46		*May*	II Sam. 23: 1–5
June	Neh. 8: 1–8		*June*	Lk. 24: 36–53
July	Mk. 4: 30–41		*July*	Acts 11: 19–26
August	Acts 28: 1–31		*August*	Jn. 7: 32–53
September	Mk. 10: 46–52		*September*	Col. 4: 1–6
October	Rev. 21: 23–27		*October*	Jn. 16: 15–33
November	Mk. 16: 15–20		*November*	Mal. 4: 1–6
December	Is. 61: 7–11		*December*	Jn. 1: 1–18

MORNING	EVENING

SUNDAY

Readings from the Psalms				*Readings from the Psalms*			
SUNDAY	1st	2nd	3rd	4th	SUNDAY	1st	2nd	3rd	4th
Jan:July	1	8	15	19	*Jan.:July*	4	23	34	43
Feb.:Aug.	24	27	29	33	*Feb.:Aug.*	84	90	91	92
Mar.:Sep.	37: 1–11	42	51: 1–10	65	*Mar.:Sep.*	102: 1–12	103: 1–14	103: 1–22	104: 1–13
Apr.:Oct.	67	95	96	97	*Apr.:Oct.*	107: 15–30	111	112	115
May:Nov.	99	100	121	124	*May:Nov.*	119: 33–40	119: 105–112	122	126
June:Dec.	128	130	133	135	*June:Dec.*	138	139	144	147